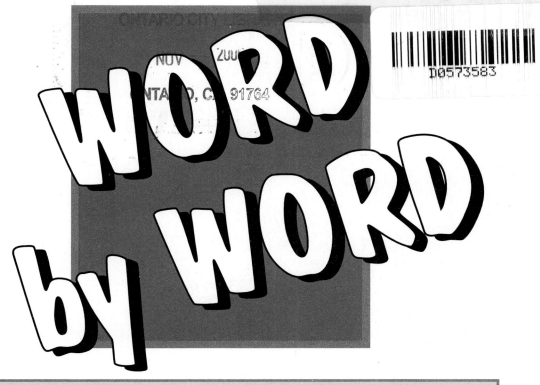

WORD by WORD

Intermediate Workbook

Steven J. Molinsky · Bill Bliss

Contributing Authors
Joan Kimball
Elizabeth Kyle

Longman

Publisher: *Tina Carver*
Director of Production and Manufacturing: *David Riccardi*
Editorial Production/Design Manager: *Dominick Mosco*
Production Supervision and Page Composition: *Ken Liao*
Electronic Art: *Todd Ware* and *Rolando Corujo*
Production Coordinator: *Ray Keating*
Cover Designer: *Merle Krumper*

Interior Design: *Kenny Beck*
Illustrations: *Richard E. Hill*

Printed in the United States of America

10   9   8   7   6

ISBN 0-13-278458-0

CONTENTS

A. WHAT'S THE QUESTION?

1. _____What's your name?_____
   Peter Alan Waterman.

2. _____
   Peter.

3. _____
   Alan.

4. _____
   Waterman.

5. _____
   16 River Road, Miami, Florida.

6. _____
   33419.

7. _____
   (407) 689-3385.

8. _____
   052-65-9027.

B. WHAT INFORMATION DO YOU NEED?

What personal information do you need to . . .

1. send a birthday present? _____name, address_____

2. make an out-of-state telephone call? _____

3. introduce two people to each other? _____

4. visit a classmate? _____

5. hire an employee? _____

C. LISTENING

Listen and choose the correct answer.

1. last name:
   a. Andrews
   b. Sands

2. first name:
   a. Andrew
   b. Stanley

3. phone number:
   a. 684-1996
   b. 844-1996

4. area code:
   a. 205
   b. 209

5. address:
   a. 14 Hudson Road in Westerly
   b. 14 Hudson Road in Easton

6. zip code:
   a. 22490
   b. 22940

A. WHO ARE THEY?

Replace the underlined words with a single word.

Here are my wedding pictures. Here's (1) my father's father. The woman next to him is (2) my father's sister. Here's (3) my mother's brother, (4) his wife, and (5) their children. Over here is (6) my sister's son, and behind him are (7) his two sisters and (8) his father. These are (9) my husband's parents. What a family!

1. my _____grandfather_____
2. my _____
3. my _____

4. my _____
5. my _____
6. my _____

7. my _____
8. my _____
9. my _____

B. RELATIVES

_c_ 1. My father's mother is my   a. son-in-law.

____ 2. My daughter's husband is my   b. niece.

____ 3. My son's son is my   c. grandmother.

____ 4. My son's wife is my   d. daughter-in-law.

____ 5. My brother's daughter is my   e. grandson.

C. WHAT'S THE RELATIONSHIP?

Using the family tree below, tell the relationships between the following people.

1. Michael : Julia _____husband : wife_____
2. Michael : Patty _____
3. Patty : Mark _____
4. Julia : Alice _____
5. Alice : Nancy

6. Edward : Nancy _____
7. Edward : Jack _____
8. Elizabeth : Chris _____
9. Anna : Patty _____
10. John : Chris _____

A. WHERE AM I?

To the north is Nebraska, to the south is Oklahoma, to the east is Missouri, and to the west is Colorado. Where am I?

1. _____Kansas_____

To the north is Canada, to the south is South Dakota, to the east is Minnesota, and to the west is Montana. Where am I?

2. _____

To the north is Nicaragua, and to the south is Panama. Where am I?

3. _____

To the north is the Yukon Territory, and to the east is Alberta. Where am I?

4. _____

To the north is Michigan, to the south is Kentucky, to the east is Ohio, and to the west is Illinois. Where am I?

5. _____

To the north is Virginia, to the south is South Carolina, to the east is the Atlantic Ocean, and to the west is Tennessee. Where am I?

6. _____

To the north is Washington, to the south is California, to the east is Idaho, and to the west is the Pacific Ocean. Where am I?

7. _____

To the north is Canada, to the south is Massachusetts, to the east is New Hampshire, and to the west is New York. Where am I?

8. _____

To the north is Arizona, to the south is Sinaloa, to the east is Chihuahua, and to the west is Baja California. Where am I?

9. _____

To the north is Arkansas, to the south is the Gulf of Mexico, to the east is Mississippi and Tennessee, and to the west is Texas. Where am I?

10. _____

To the north is Florida, to the south is Jamaica, to the east is Haiti, and to the west is Mexico. Where am I?

11. _____

To the north is New York, to the south is Maryland and West Virginia, to the east is New Jersey, and to the west is Ohio. Where am I?

12. _____

B. NORTH AMERICA GEOGRAPHY QUIZ

Try to answer the following questions without looking at the map.

1. Name the one U.S. state that isn't south of Canada.

   _____

2. Washington, Oregon, California, Alaska, and Hawaii share one common feature. What is it?

   _____

3. Janet took a trip from North Carolina to Maine. She traveled along the coast. Name the states that she passed through.

   _____

4. Tom was tired of the cold and the snow of Vermont and so he decided to take a trip along the Gulf of Mexico. Which states did he see?

   _____

5. Which U.S. states border Canada?

   _____

   _____

6. Which Canadian provinces border the U.S.?

   _____

   _____

7. Which U.S. states border the Great Lakes?

   _____

C. WHICH WAY DID THEY GO?

The Grisley Gang robbed the First National Bank and took off with the money. Which way did they go—north, south, east, or west? You decide.

1. From Utah, they passed through Colorado, Kansas, and Missouri. Which way did they go?   _____*east*_____

2. From Maine, they went through New Hampshire, Massachusetts, and Connecticut. Which way did they go?   _____

3. From Kentucky, they raced through Missouri and Kansas. Which way did they go? _____

4. From Panama, they sped through Costa Rica, Nicaragua, and El Salvador. Which way did they go?   _____

D. WHERE IN NORTH AMERICA HAVE YOU BEEN?

1. Which U.S. and Mexican states have you visited? Which Canadian provinces have you seen? Locate them on the map. . . . .

2. Which countries have you visited in Central America? . . . .

3. Which place in North America would you like most to visit? Why? . . . .

   . . . .

A. GEOGRAPHICALLY SPEAKING

1. The continent that includes Canada is _____ North America _____.

2. The long narrow country in South America with a coast on the Pacific Ocean is _____.

3. The large island off the eastern coast of southern Africa is _____.

4. The body of water between South America and Africa is the _____.

5. The _____ Ocean is between Africa and Australia.

6. The country that lies between Norway and Finland is _____.

7. The country that shares borders with the Czech Republic, Slovakia, Hungary, Slovenia, Italy, and Switzerland is _____.

8. The body of water north of Russia is the _____.

9. The two land-locked countries of South America are _____ and _____.

10. Four islands located in the Caribbean Sea are _____, _____, _____, and _____.

11. The country north of China and south of Russia is _____

12. The island off the southern coast of India is _____.

B. GEOGRAPHICAL ASSOCIATIONS

What country comes to mind when you think of . . . ?

1. silk fabrics
   The Great Wall
   Beijing

   _____ China _____

2. The Colosseum
   Leonardo da Vinci
   Venice

   _____

3. "Uncle Sam"
   The Mississippi River
   Hollywood

   _____

4. The Kremlin
   St. Petersburg
   Moscow

   _____

5. The Yukon Territory
   Hudson Bay
   Vancouver

   _____

6. Mt. Fuji
   Kyoto
   sushi

   _____

7. Sydney
   "down under"
   kangaroos

   _____

8. Taj Mahal
   Gandhi
   Bombay

   _____

9. The Sphinx
   The Great Pyramid
   Cairo

   _____

C. AROUND THE WORLD

Which country would you travel to if you wanted to . . . ?

_f_	1.	buy a samovar	a.	Germany
___	2.	visit a coffee plantation	b.	Nepal
___	3.	purchase a colorful kimono	c.	Brazil
___	4.	observe lions, giraffes, and zebras in their natural habitat	d.	United States
			e.	Panama
___	5.	visit Niagara Falls	f.	Russia
___	6.	see the temples in Bangkok	g.	Mexico
___	7.	climb Mt. Everest	h.	Japan
___	8.	view the ruins of Montezuma's empire	i.	New Zealand
___	9.	see where the Berlin Wall was	j.	Colombia
___	10.	watch ships pass through a famous canal	k.	Thailand
			l.	Portugal
___	11.	speak Portuguese in South America	m.	Kenya
			n.	Guatemala

D. CAN YOU NAME . . . ?

1. the country situated between Greenland and the United Kingdom?

_____

2. two countries whose coasts are on the Black Sea?

_____

3. three countries that have gained independence during the past decade?

_____

4. four English-speaking countries?

_____

5. five African countries?

_____

6. six countries that were formerly part of the U.S.S.R.?

_____

7. seven Spanish-speaking countries?

_____

8. all the countries that border YOUR country?

. . . .

A. WHICH WORD IS CORRECT?

1. Before she goes to bed every night, Margaret likes to (sleep   (take a bath)).

2. It's 7:00 A.M., and Mr. Jackson is making (dinner   breakfast) for his children.

3. Sharon is upset. Her boyfriend is coming in ten minutes to pick her up, and her roommate is still in the bathroom (taking a shower   eating lunch).

4. Johnny! Don't forget to (take   make) your bed before you go to school!

5. Tim flosses his (hair   teeth) after every meal.

6. Bill and Martha share the household chores. They each (make   have) dinner three nights a week.

7. Sam works in an office from 9 to 5. He likes to get to work on time. That's why he (goes to bed   gets up) at 6 A.M. every day.

8. Where's the toothpaste? I need to brush my (hair   teeth).

9. It's time to (get dressed   get undressed) and go to bed.

10. My little brother has a very short haircut because he doesn't like to (comb his hair   shave) very often.

B. LISTENING

Listen and choose the best answer.

____ get up		__1__	brush her hair
____ have lunch		____	go to bed
____ get undressed		____	shave
____ put on her makeup		____	wash her face

C. IT'S TIME TO GET UP!

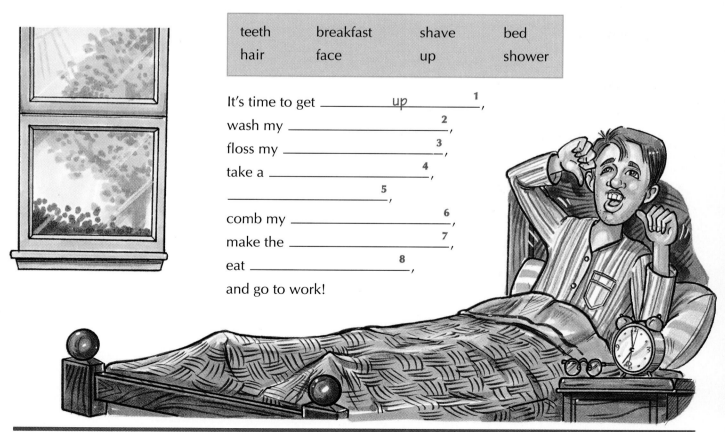

teeth	breakfast	shave	bed
hair	face	up	shower

It's time to get _____ up _____ ¹,

wash my _____ ²,

floss my _____ ³,

take a _____ ⁴,

_____ ⁵,

comb my _____ ⁶,

make the _____ ⁷,

eat _____ ⁸,

and go to work!

A. WHAT'S THE ACTIVITY?

1. Marion is busy. She's _____ *cleaning* _____ her house because guests are coming.

2. Walter is _____ the dining room furniture.

3. Joe spilled a bowl of popcorn. Now he's _____ the rug.

4. Mark's shirt is wrinkled. Now he's _____ it.

5. Tina is a concert pianist. She _____ five hours every day.

6. Jim is captain of the team. He _____ every day.

7. Keith is _____ hard for his biology test.

8. I _____ the newspaper before I go to work.

9. Fred wants to lose weight, so he _____ every morning.

10. Before television was invented, people always _____.

11. Ann has five children. She _____ every day.

12. Carl usually _____, and Janet dries them and puts them away.

B. HOW ABOUT YOU?

What have you already done today?

I've already . . . . *done the laundry.* . . . .

. . . .

. . . .

. . . .

. . . .

What haven't you done yet?

I haven't . . . . *exercised* . . . . yet.

. . . .

. . . .

. . . .

. . . .

A. FINISH THE SENTENCE

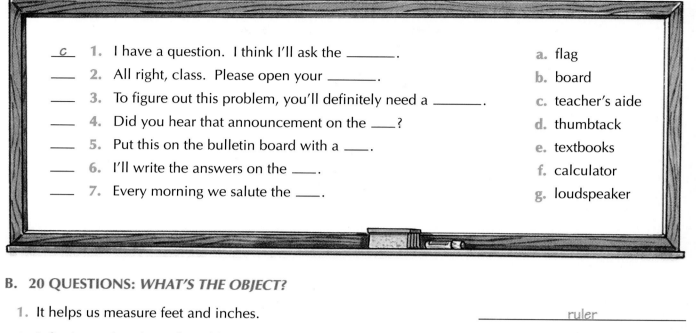

_c_	1.	I have a question. I think I'll ask the _____.	a.	flag
___	2.	All right, class. Please open your _____.	b.	board
___	3.	To figure out this problem, you'll definitely need a _____.	c.	teacher's aide
___	4.	Did you hear that announcement on the ___?	d.	thumbtack
___	5.	Put this on the bulletin board with a ___.	e.	textbooks
___	6.	I'll write the answers on the ___.	f.	calculator
___	7.	Every morning we salute the ___.	g.	loudspeaker

B. 20 QUESTIONS: *WHAT'S THE OBJECT?*

1. It helps us measure feet and inches. _____ruler_____

2. It fits in our hands, and it adds, subtracts, multiplies, and divides. _____

3. When we use it to write, we get dust on our hands. _____

4. It tells the time. _____

5. We find continents, oceans, seas, and countries on it. _____

6. I help the teacher in the classroom. _____

7. It's sharp, pointed, and very small. It can hold things up on the wall. _____

8. It has small squares on it. We use it to make charts. _____

9. It's soft and made from cloth. Every country has one. _____

10. Students and teachers use it when they aren't standing. _____

11. It's on the wall. We can hear voices through it. _____

12. It makes a sharp point on the end of a pencil. _____

13. Everybody sits at one, but the teacher's is bigger. _____

14. Students take notes and write homework assignments in it. _____

15. It's a place for dictionaries and encyclopedias when we aren't using them. _____

16. It's square and flat, and we watch movies on it. _____

17. We use it to write something in ink. _____

18. It's rectangular and gray, and it makes words on a board disappear. _____

19. It makes words written on paper disappear. _____

20. It does the work a typewriter can do, and much more. _____

A. SYNONYMS

Find the words in the second column that mean the same as the ones in the first column.

_e_   **1.** mistake
____   **2.** homework
____   **3.** book
____   **4.** lower
____   **5.** hand in
____   **6.** correct
____   **7.** turn off
____   **8.** raise
____   **9.** go over

a. assignment
b. switch off
c. look at again
d. lift up
e. error
f. pull down
g. text
h. give to a teacher
i. fix a mistake

____   **10.** take a seat
____   **11.** test
____   **12.** pair
____   **13.** group
____   **14.** chair
____   **15.** hand out
____   **16.** put away
____   **17.** erase
____   **18.** piece of paper

j. seat
k. remove
l. sit down
m. single sheet
n. two
o. exam
p. more than two
q. put in (its) place
r. distribute

B. OPPOSITE ACTIONS

1. Don't stand up! _____!

2. Don't close your textbooks! _____ them!

3. Don't turn off the lights! _____ them _____!

4. Don't put them away! _____ them _____!

5. He didn't collect the tests. He _____ them _____.

C. LISTENING

Listen and write the number of the sentence that has the same meaning.

____ Please sit down.

____ Please distribute the exams.

_1_ Please look at the errors.

____ Please give the assignment to the teacher.

____ Please put the texts in their place.

A. WHAT'S THE WORD?

Complete the following sentences using words from page 12 of the Picture Dictionary.

1. I really like music from Egypt. Unfortunately, I can't understand the words because they're all in
_____Arabic_____ .

2. My new friend is from Turkey. I love to hear her speak _____ .

3. My brother wants to go to _____ on vacation. He doesn't speak Swedish, but he loves _____ food.

4. A. Do your new neighbors come from Spain?
   B. Well, they speak _____, but actually they're from Puerto Rico. They're _____ .

5. Deborah's ancestors are from England, Denmark, Germany, and France. She is part
_____, _____, _____, and
_____ .

6. In my daughter's elementary school, there are children from Vietnam, Thailand, Brazil, and Lebanon.
They're teaching the other children _____, _____,
_____, and _____ games and customs.

7. When she was young, Jane lived in Greece, Israel, Egypt, and Taiwan. She learned a few phrases in
_____, _____, _____, and
_____ .

8. The Thompsons decided to have an international dinner. They invited their friends from Colombia,
Indonesia, Korea, and Peru. It was fantastic! They had _____,
_____, _____, and _____ food.

B. LISTENING

Listen and choose the best answer.

1. a. French
   b. English

2. a. Honduran
   b. Hungarian

3. a. Russia
   b. Poland

4. a. Spanish
   b. Costa Rican

5. a. Romanian
   b. Ukrainian

6. a. Portugal
   b. Portuguese

7. a. Malay
   b. Malaysian

8. a. Jordan
   b. Argentina

9. a. Ethiopia
   b. Pakistan

A. WHAT'S THE WORD?

cabin	condominium	dormitory	houseboat	single-family house
shelter	nursing home	farmhouse	mobile home	

1. Anna lives in a building for students on the campus of her university. She lives in a
   _____ *dormitory* _____.

2. Peter and Lucy want to rent a small log house in the mountains. They asked their real estate agent to
   find them a _____.

3. Most people who live in the suburbs live in a _____.

4. Maria wanted to own her own apartment, so she decided to look for a _____.

5. Our friends the Johnsons enjoy the water very much. That's why their new
   _____ is perfect for them.

6. On cold nights the homeless people who usually stay in the park go to the
   _____ to sleep.

7. Mr. and Mrs. Wilson retired, sold their house, and now travel around the country in their new
   _____.

8. Mike leaves the _____ every morning at 5:00 A.M. to milk the cows.

9. Mrs. Baxter is eighty years old. She's too weak to take care of herself. Her doctor thinks she should
   live in a _____.

B. ANALOGIES

Complete the analogies with a kind of housing. There may be more than one possible answer.

1. student : dormitory *as* elderly : _____ *nursing home* _____

2. countryside : farmhouse *as* river : _____

3. separate : single-family house *as* attached : _____

4. rural : farmhouse *as* urban : highrise _____

5. one : single-family house *as* two : _____

Listen and decide what kind of housing these people are talking about.

1. **a.** apartment building
   b. cabin

2. **a.** single-family house
   b. townhouse

3. **a.** farmhouse
   b. dormitory

4. **a.** shelter
   b. dormitory

5. **a.** trailer
   b. nursing home

6. **a.** condominium
   b. trailer

D. YOUR *DREAM HOUSE!*

If you had a choice, where would you like to live? Draw your *dream house* and then tell about it.

MY DREAM HOUSE BY

. . . .

. . . .

. . . .

. . . .

. . . .

. . . .

. . . .

. . . .

A. CAN YOU FIND . . . ?

Look through the list of words on page 14 of the Picture Dictionary and see if you can find . . .

3 things we sit on.

_____ armchair _____
_____
_____

5 things that use electricity.

_____
_____
_____
_____
_____

5 things to put other things on or in.

_____
_____
_____
_____
_____

6 things that are decorative.

_____
_____
_____
_____
_____
_____

2 things that reduce light.

_____
_____

5 things that are part of the structure of a house.

_____
_____
_____
_____
_____

B. WHICH WORD IS CORRECT?

1. Let's get a (CD player (VCR)) so that we can watch movies at home.
2. Would you turn on the (lamp   lampshade), please? I'm reading and I can't see.
3. The sun is in my eyes. Would you mind closing the (rug   drapes)?
4. That's a beautiful (frame   painting) on the wall. Who's the artist?
5. Michael just got a new tape to play on his (stereo system   television).
6. Do you think this (fireplace   bookcase) is big enough to hold all these textbooks?
7. We really need to buy a (coffee table   loveseat) to go in front of the couch.
   Then we can have our dessert in the living room.
8. Jane, that throw pillow looks nice on your (curtains   sofa).
9. Paul, look at that old (photograph   painting) of me! My father took it when I was two.
10. That's certainly an unusual picture frame on the (ceiling   wall)! Where did you get it?
11. We need something to hang over the (picture   mantel).
12. That (end table   coffee table) looks great next to your sofa!
13. I think that (lamp   stereo) is on too loud.
14. I just love your new wall (table   unit)!
15. We enjoy making fires in our (fireplace   fireplace screen).

A. CAN YOU FIND . . .?

Look through the list of words on page 15 of the Picture Dictionary and see if you can find . . .

4 things that hold cold beverages and foods.

_____pitcher_____

_____

_____

4 things that hold hot beverages and foods.

_____

_____

_____

2 things that hold food seasonings.

_____

_____

5 pieces of furniture.

_____

_____

_____

_____

4 things used to decorate a table.

_____

_____

_____

2 things that give light.

_____

_____

B. WHICH WORD IS CORRECT?

1. Martin, please put the fish on the serving (bowl (platter)).

2. Julie, that's a gorgeous china (cabinet   cart)!

3. Fresh flowers and fruit make a beautiful (chandelier   centerpiece).

4. Ned, please pass the butter (dish   bowl).

5. Caroline's aunt gave her a crystal (platter   pitcher) for serving lemonade.

6. Harry tripped over the (buffet   serving cart), and it rolled out of the dining room, down the hall, and into the living room.

7. We're ready to eat. Henry, would you please light the (candles   candlesticks)?

8. Ellen, there's a little salad left in the salad (shaker   bowl). Would you like some?

9. When Sally has people over for dinner, she puts all the food on the (buffet   china cabinet) and lets everyone serve themselves.

10. We keep all our best dishes in our (china   china cabinet).

11. This is a very comfortable dining room (chair   table).

12. This coffee smells wonderful! Where's the (sugar bowl   salt shaker) and (pepper shaker   creamer)?

13. Oops! I just spilled some tomato sauce on your clean white (chandelier   tablecloth)!

A. TRUE OR FALSE?

Write **T** if a statement is true and **F** if it is false.

_F_ **1.** The water glass goes to the right of the wine glass.

____ **2.** The soup bowl goes on top of the dinner plate.

____ **3.** The forks go on the right side of the dinner plate.

____ **4.** The soup spoon goes between the butter knife and the teaspoon.

____ **5.** The cup goes underneath the saucer.

____ **6.** The dinner fork is larger than the salad fork.

____ **7.** The napkin goes to the left of the dinner plate.

____ **8.** The salad plate goes to the right of the bread-and-butter plate.

B. WHAT'S THE WORD?

Fill in the correct word.

1. What lies across the bread and butter plate? _____ butter knife _____

2. What goes to the left of the dinner fork? _____

3. What do you use to cut a piece of meat? _____

4. What is folded under the forks? _____

5. What do you use for drinking coffee? _____

6. What do you use to stir coffee? _____

C. WHICH WORD DOESN'T BELONG?

1. knife	(cup)	teaspoon	fork
2. cup	butter knife	water glass	soup bowl
3. napkin	saucer	soup bowl	dinner plate
4. soup spoon	salad fork	teaspoon	water glass
5. salad plate	soup bowl	bread-and-butter plate	dinner plate

D. WHAT'S WRONG WITH THIS PLACE SETTING?

What 5 things are wrong with this place setting?

1. _The dinner fork and the salad fork are reversed._

2. _____

3. _____

4. _____

5. _____

A. LISTENING: FRED'S FURNITURE STORE

Listen to the following advertisement and write the prices you hear.

B. WHAT IS IT?

1. This tells you the time and wakes you up. _____alarm clock_____
2. These keep the sun out. _____
3. This is the first thing that goes on an unmade bed. _____
4. This keeps you warm in the winter and has a cord. _____
5. This holds earrings, bracelets, and rings. _____
6. You rest your head on this. _____
7. It's a set of twin beds, with one bed above the other. _____

C. WHAT'S THE WORD?

flat sheet	mattress	king-size bed	clock radio	fitted sheet	queen-size bed

1. Uh-oh! I forgot to plug in the _____clock radio_____.
2. Our bed has a very comfortable box spring and _____.
3. The _____ goes on top of the _____.
4. I'm looking for something larger than a _____. Do you have a _____?

D. WHICH WORD DOESN'T BELONG?

1. night table   clock radio   alarm clock   (blinds)
2. pillowcase   pillow   fitted sheet   sheet
3. chest of drawers trundle bed   clock radio   dresser
4. trundle bed   cot   electric blanket day bed
5. footboard   comforter   quilt   blanket
6. double   comforter   convertible   bunk

17

A. CAN YOU FIND . . .?

Look through the list of words on page 18 of the Picture Dictionary and see if you can find . . .

9 appliances.

_____ _dishwasher_
_____
_____
_____
_____
_____
_____
_____

5 cleaning aids.

_____
_____
_____
_____
_____

B. LISTENING

Listen and choose the best answer.

1. a. dish rack
   (b.) trash compactor

2. a. ice trays
   b. canisters

3. a. burner
   b. faucet

4. a. kitchen table
   b. cabinet

5. a. can opener
   b. pot holder

6. a. refrigerator magnet
   b. sponge

7. a. scouring pad
   b. spice rack

8. a. cookbook
   b. refrigerator

9. a. freezer
   b. toaster

C. ANALOGIES

1. garbage : garbage pail *as* paper towel : _____paper towel holder_____

2. pot holder : stove *as* dish towel : _____

3. dishes : cabinet *as* spices : _____

4. burner : oven *as* ice maker : _____

5. canisters : counter *as* refrigerator magnet : _____

6. cook : stove *as* cut : _____

7. scrub : pot scrubber *as* scour : _____

8. dishwashing liquid : sink *as* dishwasher detergent : _____

9. slow baking : oven *as* rapid baking : _____

D. WHAT'S THE OBJECT?

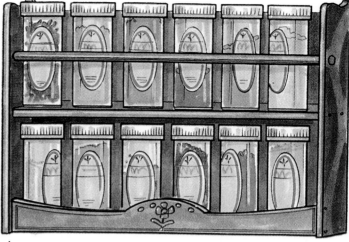

_e_ 1. scouring   **a.** opener

___ 2. cutting   **b.** rack

___ 3. spice   **c.** liquid

___ 4. can   **d.** board

___ 5. ice   **e.** pad

___ 6. dishwashing   **f.** scrubber

___ 7. pot   **g.** maker

E. WHICH WORD DOESN'T BELONG?

1. toaster   (freezer)   burner   oven

2. faucet   ice maker   burner   sink

3. dishwasher   dishwasher detergent   refrigerator   range

4. spice rack   cabinets   garbage pail   kitchen table

5. sponge   pot scrubber   potholder   scouring pad

F. WHAT'S WRONG WITH THIS KITCHEN?

Find 12 things that are strange about this kitchen.

1. _____The dishwasher is upside down._____   7. _____

2. _____   8. _____

3. _____   9. _____

4. _____   10. _____

5. _____   11. _____

6. _____   12. _____

A. EARTHQUAKE!

Mike Jensen is the manager of *Kitchen World*, a store for kitchen appliances and utensils. Last night an earthquake hit the area and shook all of the kitchenware in his store off the shelves. Can you help Mike reorganize his store? Put the items below in one of the four sections of his store: Small Electrical Appliances, Bakeware, Pots and Pans, and Small Gadgets and Utensils.

blender	electric mixer	measuring spoon	skillet
bottle opener	food processor	mixing bowl	spatula
cake pan	frying pan	paring knife	strainer
can opener	garlic press	pie plate	tea kettle
casserole dish	grater	popcorn maker	toaster oven
coffee grinder	griddle	pot	vegetable peeler
coffeemaker	ice cream scoop	pressure cooker	waffle iron
cookie sheet	knife	roaster	whisk
double boiler	ladle	roasting pan	wok
egg beater	lids	rolling pin	
electric frying pan	measuring cup	saucepan	

B. WHICH KITCHENWARE WORD IS CORRECT?

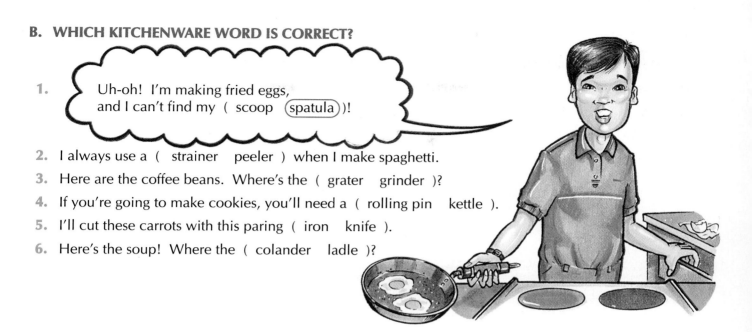

1. Uh-oh! I'm making fried eggs, and I can't find my (scoop (spatula))!

2. I always use a (strainer peeler) when I make spaghetti.
3. Here are the coffee beans. Where's the (grater grinder)?
4. If you're going to make cookies, you'll need a (rolling pin kettle).
5. I'll cut these carrots with this paring (iron knife).
6. Here's the soup! Where the (colander ladle)?

C. WHAT'S THE OBJECT?

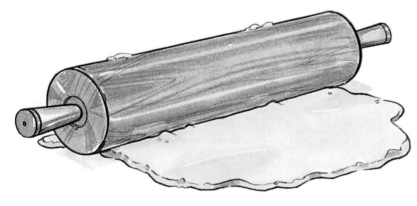

_b_	1. rolling	a.	maker
___	2. pressure	b.	pin
___	3. double	c.	kettle
___	4. tea	d.	processor
___	5. popcorn	e.	peeler
___	6. food	f.	beater
___	7. vegetable	g.	press
___	8. egg	h.	boiler
___	9. garlic	i.	cooker

D. WHICH WORD DOESN'T BELONG?

1. (ice cream scoop)   tea kettle   coffee maker   waffle iron
2. wok   saucepan   roaster   food processor
3. waffle iron   mixer   double boiler   toaster oven
4. beater   electric mixer   garlic press   whisk
5. saucepan   cake pan   pie plate   cookie sheet

E. LISTENING

Listen and choose the best answer.

1. a. wok
   b. double boiler

2. a. blender
   b. mixing bowl

3. a. measuring cup
   b. bottle opener

4. a. whisk
   b. paring knife

5. a. cookie sheet
   b. cookie cutter

6. a. lid
   b. saucepan

A. BABY WORLD

Hector and Maria are looking for the following items at *Baby World*, a store that sells everything families need for a new baby. In which department will they find the following items?

baby carriage	cradle	portable crib
booster seat	crib bumper	potty
car seat	diaper pail	stuffed animal
changing table	doll	teddy bear
chest of drawers	food warmer	walker

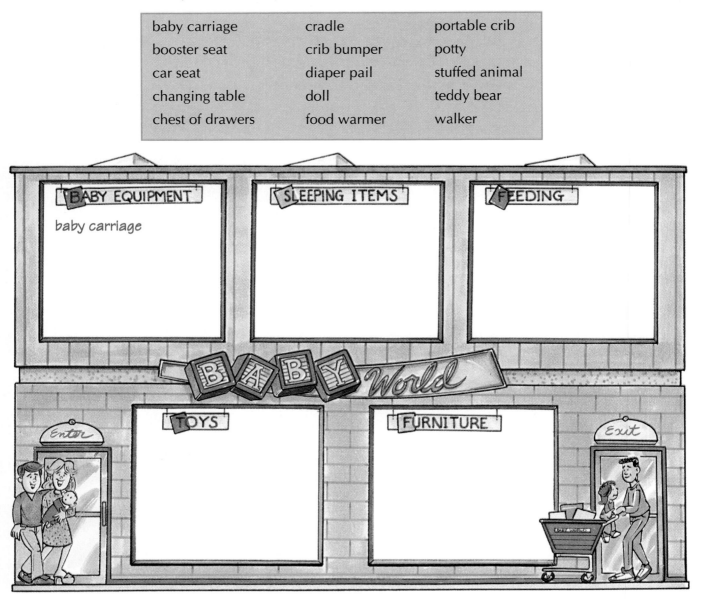

B. WHICH WORD IS CORRECT?

1. I keep all my baby's clothes in this ((chest) potty).
2. You can hear everything in the baby's room with our new (rattle   intercom).
3. Hi, sweetheart! I'm going to take you for a walk in your (mobile   stroller).
4. My little boy just loves to play with this (stuffed animal   changing table).
5. Today I think I'll dress the baby in this cute new (toy chest   stretch suit).
6. Whenever we take our baby for a ride, we put her in a (high chair   car seat).

C. CROSSWORD PUZZLE

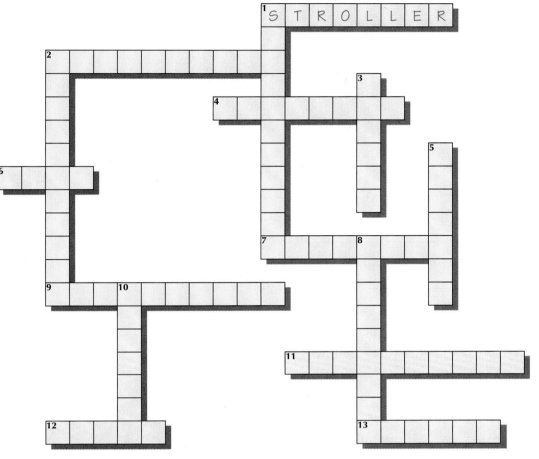

¹S T R O L L E R

ACROSS

1. You can take a baby for a walk in a _____.

2. A _____ goes inside the crib.

4. With an _____ you can hear a baby from another room.

6. A baby sleeps in a _____.

7. Toys are kept in a _____.

9. A _____ holds dirty diapers.

11. A child feels safer sleeping with a _____ on.

12. A _____ gives the baby a ride back and forth.

13. Babies like to shake a _____.

DOWN

1. An infant is often dressed in a _____.

2. A _____ goes on top of the changing table.

3. A _____ hangs over the crib.

5. Babies love to play with a _____ before napping.

8. A baby sits in a _____ while eating.

10. A _____ keeps a baby safe while playing.

A. DOCTOR'S ADVICE

pacifier	cloth diapers	diaper pins
ointment	vitamins	cotton swabs
formula	bib	baby shampoo
baby lotion	teething ring	nipples
disposable diapers		

1. If your baby has a rash, use a little _____ointment_____ .
2. When a newborn isn't nursed, it drinks _____ .
3. I feel that _____ are better for the environment.
4. When a baby wants to suck, a _____ can help.
5. A _____ is important at mealtime.
6. Cloth diapers are attached with _____ .
7. Some doctors recommend supplementing a baby's diet with _____ .
8. You should clean your infant's ears carefully with _____ .

B. ASSOCIATIONS

_e_	1. vitamins	a.	hair
___	2. diaper pins	b.	mouth
___	3. pacifier	c.	rash
___	4. baby shampoo	d.	sharp
___	5. ointment	e.	health

C. LISTENING: *WHAT ARE THEY TALKING ABOUT?*

Listen and decide what's being talked about.

___	baby shampoo
___	bib
___	diaper pins
_1_	disposable diapers
___	baby food
___	vitamins

A. PROBABLE OR IMPROBABLE?

Decide whether the following statements are probable or improbable. Mark those that are probable with a **P** and those that are improbable with an **I**.

<u>I</u> **1.** Margaret was expecting house guests, so she put fresh towels in the hamper.

_____ **2.** When the plumber came to fix the toilet, he first tried using a plunger.

_____ **3.** Vincent slipped and fell because there wasn't a bath mat in the bathtub.

_____ **4.** Cathy likes to keep a bar of soap in the soap dispenser.

_____ **5.** The plumber told us we needed a new vanity for our drain.

_____ **6.** My washcloth is smaller than my bath towel.

_____ **7.** John turned on the air freshener because the bathroom was hot.

_____ **8.** I weigh myself every day on my scale.

_____ **9.** Jill cleans the toilet with a Water Pic.

_____ **10.** Gary dries his hair with a fan.

_____ **11.** My doctor says it's important to take this medicine chest every day.

B. WHAT'S THE OBJECT?

<u>d</u> **1.** toothbrush   **a.** dispenser

_____ **2.** soap   **b.** mat

_____ **3.** shower   **c.** cabinet

_____ **4.** hand   **d.** holder

_____ **5.** rubber   **e.** head

_____ **6.** medicine   **f.** towel

_____ **7.** towel   **g.** rack

C. WHAT'S THE ACTION?

Decide which actions are associated with the following objects. There may be more than one possible answer.

a. toilet	**e.** air freshener	**i.** faucet
b. cup	**f.** towel	**j.** sponge
c. scale	**g.** facecloth	**k.** drain
d. tub	**h.** medicine cabinet	

<u>c</u> **1.** weigh   _____ **6.** turn on   _____ **11.** leak

_____ **2.** flush   _____ **7.** squeeze   _____ **12.** fold

_____ **3.** spray   _____ **8.** open   _____ **13.** turn off

_____ **4.** fill   _____ **9.** wash   _____ **14.** clog

_____ **5.** sit   _____ **10.** store   _____ **15.** drink

A. WHAT'S USED WHERE?

Match the following items with a part of the body. There may be more than one possible answer.

a. lipstick	**e.** conditioner	**i.** shaving creme	**m.** blush
b. dental floss	**f.** bobby pins	**j.** styptic pencil	**n.** barrettes
c. tweezers	**g.** eye shadow	**k.** shampoo	**o.** mascara
d. deodorant	**h.** after shave lotion	**l.** makeup	**p.** nail polish

___g___ **1.** eyelids   _____ **3.** hair   _____ **5.** mouth   _____ **7.** face

_____ **2.** underarms   _____ **4.** eyebrows   _____ **6.** eyelashes   _____ **8.** fingers

B. WHICH WORD IS CORRECT?

1. Ouch! I just broke a nail. Do you have a nail ((file) brush)?
2. My shoes look dull. I need to find some shoe (polish   spray) to shine them.
3. After her shower, Gina likes to put on some (styptic pencil   powder).
4. Ever since Tom grew a beard, he hasn't bought any (after shave lotion   cologne).
5. Some women with thick eyebrows pluck them with (scissors   tweezers).
6. Jennifer wants her blonde eyelashes to look darker, so she uses (makeup   mascara).
7. This color is too bright. I need to take it off with (nail polish remover   nail polish).
8. This razor isn't working very well. I think the (shaver   blade) is dull.
9. The baby is scratching me with her fingernails. Do you have a nail (brush   clipper) that I can use to cut them?

C. WHICH WORD DOESN'T BELONG?

1. toothbrush	(deodorant)	mouthwash	dental floss
2. conditioner	foundation	brush	comb
3. after shave lotion	razor	blades	shaving creme
4. lipstick	mascara	eyeliner	styptic pencil
5. nail file	nail clipper	tweezers	scissors

D. ANALOGIES

1. nails : nail polish *as* shoes : _____shoe polish_____
2. conditioner : rinse *as* perfume : _____
3. styptic : pencil *as* dental : _____
4. brush : comb *as* nail file : _____
5. razor : shaving creme *as* toothbrush : _____

A. WHAT DOES NICK NEED?

Nick is cleaning his apartment and doing his laundry. Decide what he needs in order to do his chores. There may be more than one possible answer.

__d__	**1.**	to make his wrinkled clothes smooth
_____	**2.**	to sweep the kitchen floor
_____	**3.**	to clean the wall-to-wall carpet
_____	**4.**	to wash the kitchen floor
_____	**5.**	to get stains out of his white shirts
_____	**6.**	to make his clothes soft
_____	**7.**	to make his shirts stiff
_____	**8.**	to clean his windows and mirrors
_____	**9.**	to do the laundry
_____	**10.**	to put the trash in
_____	**11.**	to wipe spilled milk
_____	**12.**	to make his wooden furniture shiny
_____	**13.**	to hang his clothes out to dry
_____	**14.**	to put his ironed shirts in the closet

a.	fabric softener
b.	furniture polish
c.	bleach
d.	iron
e.	broom
f.	detergent
g.	clothesline
h.	sponge
i.	sponge mop
j.	starch
k.	window cleaner
l.	garbage can
m.	paper towels
n.	clothespins
o.	hangers
p.	vacuum

B. LISTENING

Listen and choose the best answer.

1. **a.** clothespins
   b. clothesline

2. **a.** carpet sweeper
   b. feather duster

3. **a.** dryer
   b. cleanser

4. **a.** scrub brush
   b. utility sink

5. **a.** sponge
   b. sponge mop

6. **a.** spray starch
   b. ammonia

C. ANALOGIES

1. laundry : laundry basket *as* garbage : _____garbage can_____

2. furniture : furniture polish *as* floor : _____

3. vacuum cleaner attachments : vacuum cleaner *as* clothespins : _____

4. bucket : pail *as* dust mop : _____

5. vacuum : hand vacuum *as* broom : _____

A. ASSOCIATIONS

_d_ 1. mailbox   a. car
___ 2. doorbell   b. relax
___ 3. grill   c. rain
___ 4. garage   d. letters
___ 5. lawn chair   e. hamburgers
___ 6. gutter   f. ring

B. WHAT'S THE OBJECT?

1. A. What does a _____lamppost_____ do?
   B. It lights up the front of your house.

2. A. Why do people have an _____ on their roof?
   B. It helps the TV get better reception.

3. A. What's a _____ used for?
   B. It keeps the grass from getting too high.

4. A. Why is a _____ useful to have?
   B. It's a good place to store garden equipment.

5. A. Why do many houses have _____s?
   B. They're used as a window decoration.

6. A. What's a _____ used for?
   B. It's used to cook food outside the home.

7. A. What's a _____ used for?
   B. It's a place to keep your car.

8. A. What's a _____ for?
   B. It carries rain water from the gutter to the ground.

9. A. Why do houses in northern climates have a _____?
   B. It helps to keep the cold air out.

10. A. What's a _____ used for?
    B. It lets you know that someone is at the door.

11. A. What's the purpose of a _____?
    B. It's a place for smoke from the fireplace to go.

12. A. Why do people like having _____s and _____s?
    B. They're great places to relax outside and enjoy the fresh air.

C. WHICH WORD IS CORRECT?

1. Last night's storm knocked the TV antenna off the ((roof) doorknob).

2. It's such a warm evening. Let's have a barbecue on the (deck   driveway).

3. Since they got a (satellite dish   side door), the Smiths can watch TV programs from all over the world.

4. During the winter months we keep the (front walk   storm door) closed.

5. You'd better close the (garage   screen). Bugs are coming in the window!

6. Rain water goes into the gutter, down the (drainpipe   patio), and onto the ground.

D. LISTENING: *WHAT ARE THEY TALKING ABOUT?*

Listen and decide what's being talked about.

1. a. front walk
   b. back door

2. a. chimney
   b. patio

3. a. gutters
   b. screens

4. a. toolshed
   b. front porch

5. a. roof
   b. lamppost

6. a. front light
   b. front door

E. WHAT'S WRONG WITH THIS HOUSE?

List 9 things that are very strange about this house.

1. _____ The mailbox is on the roof. _____   6. _____

2. _____   7. _____

3. _____   8. _____

4. _____   9. _____

5. _____

MY FIRST APARTMENT

Complete the following letter using words from page 26 of the Picture Dictionary.

Dear Mom and Dad,

   Guess what! I moved into my first apartment. It's fantastic! Let me tell you about it. First of all, there's an Olympic-sized _____swimming pool_____ [1] and heated _____ [2] to swim and relax in. I don't need to worry about parking because there's a _____ [3] behind the building. And don't worry! This building is very secure. There's a 24-hour _____ [4] on duty in the _____ [5] and a _____ [6] and a _____ [7] on the door to my apartment. If someone comes to visit, they ring the _____ [8] and I can talk to them through the _____ [9]. When they knock on the door, I always look through the _____ [10] just to make sure who it is. My apartment is on the eighth floor. Luckily there's an _____ [11] so I don't have to climb up all those stairs. In the basement there's a _____ [12] with a new washer and dryer and a _____ [13] where I can keep my skis and bicycle. There are _____ [14]s on the ceilings of all the rooms. They go off when I burn my dinner! I have an _____ [15] in my bedroom to keep me cool in the summer, and there's even a _____ [16] where I can sit when the weather is nice. The _____ [17] lives in the building, so if I have any problems, she's always available to help. I hope you'll visit soon.

                                        Love,
                                        Carmen

A. WHO TO CALL?

Victor just bought a very old house that needs a lot of work. Tell him who to call when . . .

1. his refrigerator doesn't keep food cold.   _appliance repair person_

2. black smoke comes out of the fireplace when it's being used.   _____

3. his kitchen is infested with cockroaches.   _____

4. the dining room needs cabinets and shelves.   _____

5. the exterior paint is chipped and peeling.   _____

6. he has a broken window.   _____

7. the key doesn't work in the front door.   _____

8. the shrubs, flowerbeds, and lawn are overgrown.   _____

9. the drain in his kitchen sink backs up.   _____

10. he can't watch his favorite TV program because
    his TV isn't working.   _____

B. LISTENING: *WHAT ARE THEY TALKING ABOUT?*

Listen and decide who or what's being talked about.

___ plumber	___ TV repair person	___ gardener
___ parking fee	___ handyman	___ pest control bill
___ oil bill	___ mortgage payment	___ locksmith
_1_ rent	___ telephone bill	

C. PAYING THE BILLS

Complete the following using words from page 27 of the Picture Dictionary.

A. I can't believe how high our _____telephone bill_____ [1] is this month! We must have made a lot of calls to our families in Brazil.

B. Hmm. You're right.

A. And look at our _____ [2]! I guess we took too many long showers.

B. I guess we did.

A. What about our _____ [3]? We can't keep the air conditioner on so much.

B. I agree. And you know something? I don't think we should pay this _____ [4] since there are still ants everywhere!

A. You're right. Let's not pay it.

B. Tell me, do you think we should switch to gas heat? Our _____ [5] is unbelievably high this month!

A. Hmm. Maybe we should think about it.

B. And look! The _____ [6] is due. I guess we'd better pay it before we start getting parking tickets.

A. I guess we should.

B. Oh, no! Wait until you see this! The _____ [7] went up, and the landlord didn't even tell us.

A. Are you serious?!

B. Yes, I am. But you know, it's still cheaper than if we bought a house and had to make a _____ [8] to a loan company every month!

A. I guess you're right.

B. Paying bills is depressing!

A. It sure is!

32

A. CAN YOU FIND . . . ?

Look through the list of words on page 28 of the Picture Dictionary and see if you can find . . .

4 tools for cutting.

_____
_____
_____
_____

3 tools for making holes.

_____
_____
_____

12 tools and supplies for fastening and unfastening.

_____   _____
_____   _____
_____   _____
_____   _____
_____   _____
_____   _____

7 tools and equipment for painting.

_____
_____
_____
_____
_____
_____
_____

B. WHICH WORD IS CORRECT?

1. Hand me the (level (hammer)). I need to bang in this nail.
2. Be careful with that (saw   nut)! You might cut yourself.
3. You can tighten that (plane   bolt) with this (chisel   wrench).
4. The best way to make this piece of wood smooth is to use a (hatchet   plane).
5. Here! You can get the paint off with this (scraper   monkey wrench).
6. The only way to clamp these two pieces of wood together is by using a (washer   vise).

C. LISTENING: WHICH TOOL IS IT?

Listen to the sounds. Write the number next to the tool you hear.

____ power saw		____ saw	
____ sandpaper		_1_ hammer	
____ scraper		____ electric drill	

A. ASSOCIATIONS

_i_	1. flashlight	a.	water
___	2. sprinkler	b.	leaves
___	3. work gloves	c.	hole
___	4. rake	d.	insect
___	5. extension cord	e.	hands
___	6. yardstick	f.	toilet
___	7. plunger	g.	inch
___	8. mousetrap	h.	plug
___	9. shovel	i.	dark
___	10. fly swatter	j.	grass
___	11. lawnmower	k.	mice

B. WHICH WORD IS CORRECT?

1. Oh, no! The electricity went out! Where's the ((flashlight)   light bulb)?

2. It must have snowed a foot last night. We'd better get the (wheelbarrow   shovel).

3. This flower bed is so dry! I need the (watering can   vegetable seeds).

4. We need an (extension cord   electrical tape) in order to plug in this lamp.

5. On a hot summer day, the children like to run through the (sprinkler   mousetrap).

6. We could use a (rake   step ladder) to gather up all these leaves.

7. The rosebush is starting to block the window. I'll trim it with the new (plunger   hedge clippers) we bought the other day.

8. We love our new (garden hose   yardstick). It's long enough to reach every part of the lawn.

9. It's a good idea to wear (fertilizer   work gloves) when you do the gardening.

10. That squeaky old door just needs some (fuses   oil) and it'll be like new again.

11. In the hot humid weather, when there are lots of bugs around, it's necessary to have a good (step ladder   fly swatter).

12. The dog has dug up the lawn! Could you pick up some (grass seed   batteries) at the store?

C. LISTENING: *WHAT ARE THEY TALKING ABOUT?*

Listen and decide what's being talked about.

___	mouse trap
___	insect spray
_1_	hedge clippers
___	glue
___	lawnmower
___	fertilizer

C. CROSSWORD PUZZLE

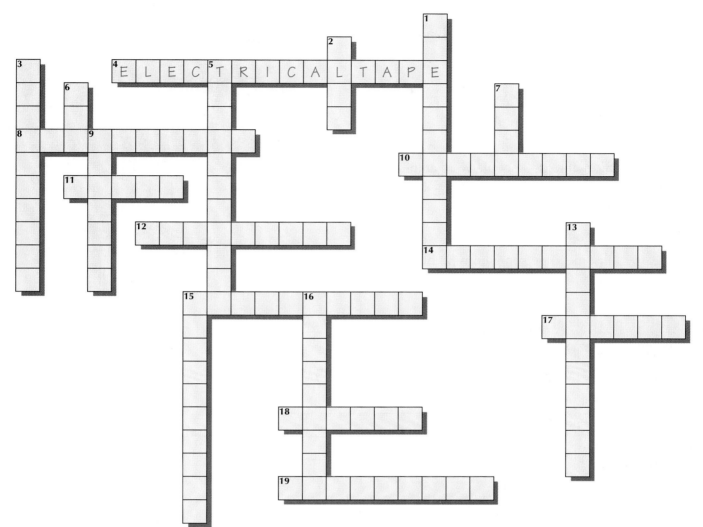

ELECTRICALTAPE

ACROSS

4. You might wrap this around a broken wire.
8. This helps you reach high places.
10. A portable radio won't work without these.
11. Without these, your electricity won't work.
12. You catch rodents with this.
14. These keep your hands clean when gardening.
15. This makes things that grow become healthier.
17. You use this to dig a hole.
18. It's usually at one end of a hose.
19. Planting this will turn your yard into a lawn.

DOWN

1. You can fill this up with leaves and wheel it away.
2. This sticks things together.
3. You kill flies with this.
5. You use this to find the length of something.
6. This is a gardening tool.
7. The sprinkler is attached to this.
9. This helps unclog a toilet.
13. This kills one kind of insect.
15. This is useful if the electricity fails.
16. This keeps the grass low.

A. LISTENING: *SAME OR DIFFERENT?*

As you listen to the following sentences, read the sentences written below. Write **S** if the sentences are the same or **D** if the sentences are different.

__D__ **1.** Carol's phone number is 365-0781.

____ **2.** Bill's zip code is 49209.

____ **3.** Ellen lives at 759 Massachusetts Avenue.

____ **4.** Joseph's office number is (503) 572-8815.

____ **5.** Lisa's social security number is 007-52-7769.

____ **6.** Last night 2000 people were at the baseball game.

____ **7.** Chris invited 50 people to his New Year's party.

____ **8.** Hal's new Toyota cost $14,589.

____ **9.** The population of our town is 2800.

____ **10.** I just met a person who is 58 but looks 18!

B. ORDINALS

Change the cardinal numbers in parentheses into ordinal numbers.

1. Henry, is that your (5) _____fifth_____ piece of apple pie?

2. Jill Stevens came in (2) _____ in this year's race for mayor.

3. Martha just gave birth to her (4) _____ son.

4. Sally's grandmother is celebrating her (90) _____ birthday today.

5. The Martins just celebrated their (50) _____ wedding anniversary.

6. On the (1) _____ day of April, many people play jokes on each other.

7. On the (27) _____ of March, we're going to Florida for vacation.

8. Barbara and George live on the (49) _____ floor of a highrise apartment building.

9. For Miriam's (36) _____ birthday, her husband gave her a new watch.

10. Johnny! That's the (8) _____ time I've told you to clean up your room!

C. WHAT'S THE NUMBER?

1. I live on the tenth floor and Barbara lives on the twentieth floor. Her apartment is on a ((higher) lower) floor.

2. My birthday is on the fifth of May. My brother's is on the fifteenth of May. We celebrate (my his) birthday first each year.

3. Seventeen is a (higher lower) number than seventy.

4. Louise and Donald have been married for half a century. I can't believe they're celebrating their (fifth fiftieth) anniversary this year!

5. I'm so excited! I scored in the (ninth ninetieth) percentile on the test!

6. My son is going to graduate from high school this year. He's in the (twelfth twentieth) grade.

7. I can vote in the next election! I'm going to be (twenty-first twenty-one) soon.

8. This is the (ten tenth) time I've told you to take out the garbage, Howard!

A. ARITHMETIC

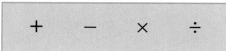

Decide which sign you need to answer the following arithmetic problems.

1. 18 [−] 12 = 6
2. 24 [ ] 2 = 12
3. 5 [ ] 3 = 15

4. 8 [ ] 8 = 64
5. 30 [ ] 2 = 32
6. 22 [ ] 2 = 11

7. 3 [ ] 3 = 9
8. 7 [ ] 4 = 3
9. 12 [ ] 9 = 21

Now practice saying the problems.

B. LISTENING: *FRACTIONS*

Listen to the following recipe. Write **C** if George has put in the correct amount of the ingredients or **I** if George has put in the incorrect amount.

_C_ 1. 2/3 of a cup of sugar

____ 2. 2/3 of a cup of oil

____ 3. 2 eggs

____ 4. 2 1/4 cups of flour

____ 5. 1 teaspoon of baking powder

____ 6. 1/3 of a teaspoon of salt

____ 7. 1 3/4 cups of crushed walnuts

____ 8. 3 ripe bananas

C. PERCENTS

Jerry and Carol Brown love bargains! That's why they were so excited about the big sale at Grant's Department Store last weekend. How much did they spend on the following items?

1. $70 lamp—50% off $35.00
2. $150 suit—40% off   _____
3. $30 shirt—10% off   _____
4. $160 silk dress—25% off   _____
5. $20 jersey—30% off   _____
6. $1250 dining room table—40% off   _____
7. $290 piece of luggage—half price   _____
8. $19 beach towel—70% off   _____
9. $189 bicycle—50% off   _____

A. WHAT TIME IS IT?

Write the time below each of the following clocks. If there is more than one way to tell the time, give both ways.

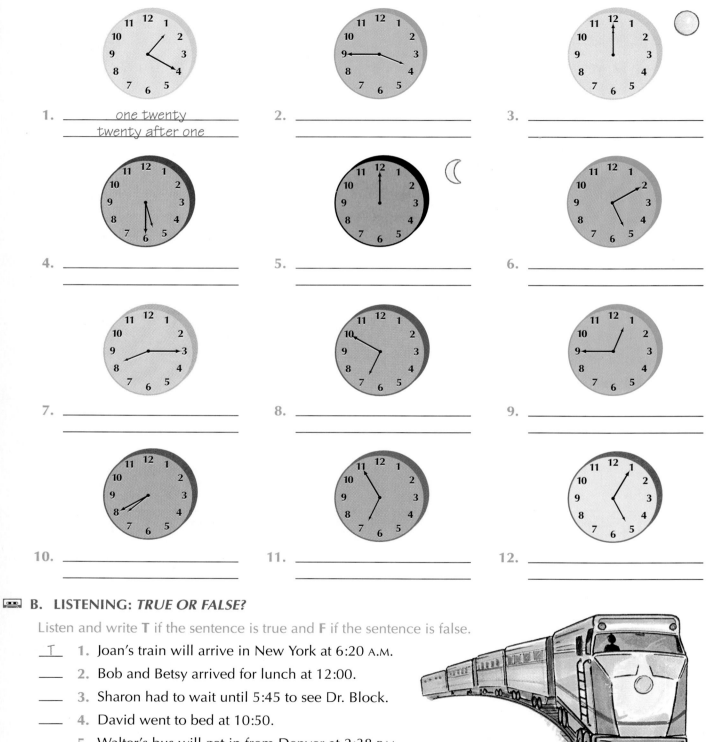

1. _____one twenty_____
   _____twenty after one_____

2. _____

3. _____

4. _____

5. _____

6. _____

7. _____

8. _____

9. _____

10. _____

11. _____

12. _____

B. LISTENING: *TRUE OR FALSE?*

Listen and write **T** if the sentence is true and **F** if the sentence is false.

__T__ 1. Joan's train will arrive in New York at 6:20 A.M.

_____ 2. Bob and Betsy arrived for lunch at 12:00.

_____ 3. Sharon had to wait until 5:45 to see Dr. Block.

_____ 4. David went to bed at 10:50.

_____ 5. Walter's bus will get in from Denver at 2:38 P.M.

_____ 6. John has an appointment to see Professor Cates at 4:10.

_____ 7. Margaret babysat from 10:00 A.M. until 11:30 P.M.

A. U.S. CALENDAR QUIZ

What do you know about the following U.S. dates?

1. On the first day of _____April_____, people often play tricks and jokes on each other.

2. Sweethearts celebrate Valentine's Day with cards, candy, and flowers in _____.

3. On the _____ of _____, Americans celebrate their independence with fireworks and parades.

4. Many people make resolutions and promises of what they will do differently on the first day of _____.

5. "_____ Night Live" is a popular weekly TV show.

6. Americans honor workers on Labor Day and autumn officially begins in _____.

7. "_____ showers bring _____ flowers" is a famous saying.

8. Summer begins in _____, and many people celebrate Father's Day in this month.

9. For most people, _____ marks the first day of the work week.

10. In _____, Americans celebrate Thanksgiving with a festive holiday meal.

B. IN MY COUNTRY . . .

1. . . . . is usually the hottest month of the year and . . . . is usually the coldest.

2. The wettest month of the year is typically . . . .

3. We celebrate our independence on the . . . . of . . . .

4. Most schools begin in . . . . and end in . . . .

5. We honor and celebrate mothers on a day in . . . . , fathers on a day in . . . . , and children on a day in . . . .

6. The work week for most people ends on . . . .

7. We remember and honor the dead on the . . . . of . . . .

8. Most people take vacations in . . . . because . . . .

C. IMPORTANT DATES IN MY LIFE

What are some important dates in your life – such as your birthday, your anniversary, the date you moved to a new city or country, or started a new job?

Important Dates	The Occasion
. . . .	. . . .
. . . .	. . . .
. . . .	. . . .
. . . .	. . . .
. . . .	. . . .

A. WHERE CAN I GET . . .?

Using the places on pages 34–37 of the Picture Dictionary, decide where you can get the following things. There may be more than one possible answer.

Where can I get . . .

1. a new suit?   _clothing store/department store/discount store_
2. my car fixed?   _____
3. my hair washed and cut?   _____
4. airplane tickets?   _____
5. a medical prescription filled?   _____
6. the oil in my car changed?   _____
7. a pair of sneakers and high heels?   _____
8. a quart of milk?   _____
9. a hammer and nails?   _____
10. a birthday cake?   _____
11. a ham and cheese sandwich?   _____
12. a kitten?   _____
13. a bouquet of tulips and daffodils?   _____
14. a workout?   _____
15. a stuffed animal?   _____
16. a hot fudge sundae?   _____
17. a good novel?   _____
18. a blood test and a physical exam?   _____
19. prescription sunglasses?   _____
20. my wool clothes cleaned and pressed?   _____
21. a fancy dinner?   _____
22. a massage?   _____
23. a shave?   _____
24. a ticket to Cleveland?   _____
25. a book of stamps?   _____
26. a silver bracelet?   _____
27. a computer?   _____
28. a food processor?   _____
29. a cup of coffee?   _____
30. traveler's checks and foreign currency?   _____

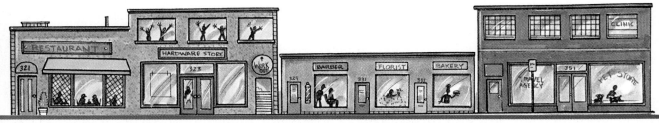

B. WHERE CAN I . . .?

Using the places on pages 34-37 of the Picture Dictionary, decide where you can do the following things. There may be more than one possible answer.

Where can I . . .

1. hear classical music?   _____ *concert hall* _____
2. see a James Bond film?   _____
3. play softball?   _____
4. see an exhibit of modern art?   _____
5. see a giraffe?   _____
6. fly a kite?   _____
7. get some film developed quickly?   _____
8. wash and dry my clothes?   _____
9. buy a dress for my pregnant sister?   _____
10. rent a new movie?   _____

C. WHICH WORD DOESN'T BELONG?

1. auto dealer	(park)	parking garage	gas station
2. pizza shop	coffee shop	barber shop	ice cream shop
3. concert hall	music store	night club	copy center
4. hotel	motel	hospital	convenience store
5. computer store	drug store	movie theater	video store
6. train station	bus station	service station	photo shop
7. hair salon	shoe store	clothing store	maternity shop
8. school	zoo	child-care center	coffee shop
9. bus station	travel agency	vision center	train station
10. cleaners	library	child-care center	shoe store

D. ANALOGIES

1. potato salad : deli *as* donuts :   _____ *donut shop* _____
2. earrings : jewelry shop *as* poodle :   _____
3. shoes : shoe store *as* videos :   _____
4. flower shop : florist *as* spa :   _____
5. shop : shopping mall *as* park :   _____
6. books : library *as* paintings :   _____
7. teacher : school *as* musician :   _____
8. restaurant : cafeteria *as* hotel :   _____
9. copy machines : copy center *as* washing machines :   _____

WHAT'S THE WORD?

Complete the following using words from pages 38-39 of the Picture Dictionary.

1. I smell smoke! Where's the nearest _____<u>fire alarm</u>_____?

2. There's the _____. I hope she didn't give us a ticket. I forgot to put money in the _____.

3. Ted is in a hurry to get to the airport. Is there a _____ near here?

4. The streets near the park are dark and dangerous. The city really needs to install more _____s.

5. When motorists see _____s at _____s, they should stop and let them walk across the street.

6. Tom just went to the _____ to buy a magazine.

7. My feet are killing me! Let's sit on that _____ until the subway comes.

8. Did you remember to put out the trash? I think I hear the _____.

9. It's raining cats and dogs! Fortunately, the bank has a _____ so we won't have to get out of the car.

10. It's important to park the car close to the _____.

11. The judge and the lawyer are on their way to work at the _____.

12. I wonder what's keeping Steve? He's over an hour late. Let's find a _____ and call him.

13. Janet was late for Bob's party because she couldn't read the _____ on the _____ where Bob's house is located.

14. Jim is an architect and works on the top floor of a modern _____. Lawyers, dentists, doctors, graphic designers, and accountants all work there, too.

15. The streets are full of litter! The city really needs to put out a lot more _____s.

A. WHAT'S THE CATEGORY?

_f_	1. size	a.	thick–thin
___	2. weight	b.	noisy–quiet
___	3. speed	c.	hot–cold
___	4. texture	d.	heavy–thin
___	5. age	e.	fast–slow
___	6. thickness	f.	tall–short
___	7. temperature	g.	handsome–ugly
___	8. price	h.	young–old
___	9. attractiveness	i.	expensive–cheap
___	10. sound	j.	smooth–rough

B. THE RIGHT WORD

Choose the adjective that best describes each of the groups below.

bad	dry	high	low
clean	fast	hot	soft
difficult	full	loud	thick

1. _____fast_____
train
runner
watch

2. _____
skin
cushion
toothbrush

3. _____
grade
temperature
altitude

4. _____
music
party
person

5. _____
situation
test
problem

6. _____
hair
accent
line

7. _____
dishes
clothes
climate

8. _____
desk
hands
house

9. _____
glass
person
room

10. _____
voice
bridge
heels

11. _____
weather
coffee
temper

12. _____
weather
grades
luck

C. SYNONYMS

Match the following synonyms. Careful! Each word in the box may have more than one synonym in the list below.

a. beautiful	**d.** dirty	**g.** neat	**j.** thin
b. clean	**e.** heavy	**h.** small	**k.** ugly
c. closed	**f.** hot	**i.** tall	**l.** wide

____l____ 1. broad

_____ 2. chubby

_____ 3. diminutive

_____ 4. filthy

_____ 5. gorgeous

_____ 6. hideous

_____ 7. immaculate

_____ 8. homely

_____ 9. lanky

_____ 10. meticulous

_____ 11. petite

_____ 12. scalding

_____ 13. shut

_____ 14. slender

_____ 15. stout

D. "SKY HIGH!"

See if you can figure out the correct combination of the following words. The meaning is always "very"— i.e., "sky high" means "very high."

ice	brand	dirt	sky	razor	boiling
bone	chock	filthy	pitch	skin	sparkling

1. "____sky____ high"

2. "_____ cheap"

3. "_____ cold"

4. "_____ dark"

5. "_____ dry"

6. "_____ full"

7. "_____ rich"

8. "_____ hot"

9. "_____ new"

10. "_____ sharp"

11. "_____ clean"

12. "_____ tight"

E. LISTENING

Listen and choose the best answer.

1. (a.) loose
   b. tight

2. a. straight
   b. crooked

3. a. wide
   b. narrow

4. a. open
   b. closed

5. a. sharp
   b. dull

6. a. thin
   b. thick

7. a. shiny
   b. dull

8. a. empty
   b. full

9. a. wet
   b. dry

10. a. hard
    b. soft

11. a. easy
    b. difficult

12. a. young
    b. old

A. WHICH WORD DOESN'T BELONG?

1. pleased   ecstatic   (shocked)   happy
2. tired   proud   sleepy   exhausted
3. nervous   furious   angry   mad
4. upset   annoyed   bored   frustrated
5. full   hungry   thirsty   jealous

B. ANALOGIES

1. angry : furious *as* tired : _____ exhausted _____
2. angry : mad *as* scared : _____
3. hot : cold *as* pleased : _____
4. hungry : full *as* ashamed : _____
5. disgusting : disgusted *as* shocking : _____

C. THE NEXT WORD

See if you can figure out which prepositions these adjectives are followed by.

1. furious   _b, c, e_   **a.** of
2. jealous   _____   **b.** about
3. worried   _____   **c.** at
4. pleased   _____   **d.** by
5. shocked   _____   **e.** with

D. SYNONYMS

Match the following synonyms.

_d_   1. afraid   **a.** bloated
____   2. cold   **b.** famished
____   3. confused   **c.** perplexed
____   4. ecstatic   **d.** petrified
____   5. exhausted   **e.** seething
____   6. full   **f.** shivering
____   7. furious   **g.** thrilled
____   8. hungry   **h.** wiped out

E. WHICH WORD IS CORRECT?

1. After running in the Boston Marathon, Kim was ((exhausted) ashamed).

2. James is having trouble finding a job. He's feeling very (ecstatic   frustrated).

3. After eating several pieces of his girlfriend's delicious apple pie, Juan was (full   furious).

4. Richard feels (cold   confused) when his English teacher speaks too quickly.

5. When Sara and Paul's daughter graduated from medical school, they felt extremely (proud   hungry).

6. The spoiled meat made all the guests (sick   hot).

7. I can't believe you did that! I'm really (bored   shocked)!

8. I don't think you should marry Charles. You'll be (ecstatic   miserable) for the rest of your life!

9. Don't be (exhausted   embarrassed) if you don't know the answer. We all make mistakes.

F. LISTENING: *HOW ARE THEY FEELING?*

Listen and choose the best description of the person's feelings.

1. a. She must be exhausted.
   b. She must be proud.

2. a. He's quite pleased.
   b. He's absolutely furious.

3. a. He was miserable.
   b. He was full.

4. a. She's confused.
   b. She's sick.

5. a. I'm sure you're disappointed.
   b. I'm sure you're nervous.

6. a. You must be jealous.
   b. You must be ecstatic.

7. a. She's probably embarrassed.
   b. She's probably nervous.

8. a. He's completely confused.
   b. He's totally bored.

G. "FREEZING COLD!"

See if you can figure out the following expressions. The meaning is always "very." For example, "freezing cold" means "very cold."

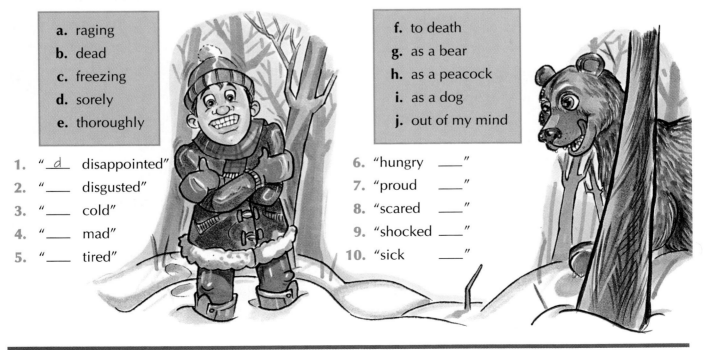

a.	raging
b.	dead
c.	freezing
d.	sorely
e.	thoroughly

f.	to death
g.	as a bear
h.	as a peacock
i.	as a dog
j.	out of my mind

1. " _d_ disappointed"
2. "___ disgusted"
3. "___ cold"
4. "___ mad"
5. "___ tired"

6. "hungry ___"
7. "proud ___"
8. "scared ___"
9. "shocked ___"
10. "sick ___"

46

A. WHAT'S THE FRUIT?

a. banana	**f.** orange
b. coconut	**g.** peach
c. cranberry	**h.** pineapple
d. grape	**i.** raisin
e. lemon	**j.** watermelon

_c_ 1. This hard, red berry is an important part of the U.S. Thanksgiving celebration.

____ 2. This citrus fruit is high in Vitamin C and is a popular breakfast juice.

____ 3. This very sour, yellow citrus fruit makes your mouth pucker.

____ 4. This soft, yellow fruit is eaten by both people and monkeys.

____ 5. This large, oval-shaped fruit is red inside with black seeds.

____ 6. This red-orange and yellow fruit has furry skin and a large pit.

____ 7. This fruit comes in bunches and may be green, purple, or red.

____ 8. This small, dark brown dried fruit used to be number 7.

____ 9. This rough-skinned fruit is sweet and yellow inside and is grown in Hawaii.

____ 10. Many people like to drink the *milk* inside this tropical fruit.

B. WHICH FRUIT?

1. If you like citrus fruits, you'll love this (papaya (orange)).
2. Can I have a piece of that (avocado   blueberry) pie?
3. I need to peel this (apricot   banana).
4. When you're at the grocery store, please pick up a few bunches of (grapes   raspberries).
5. I almost can't tell the difference between an orange and a (tangerine   plum).
6. I was so hungry I ate half of the (raisin   watermelon).

C. "THE APPLE OF MY EYE!"

See if you can figure out the meanings of the following expressions containing *fruit* words.

1. You're the apple of my eye!
   a. You bother me.
   b. You're my favorite.

2. He's a real peach!
   a. He's a wonderful person.
   b. His skin is very soft.

3. That's just sour grapes!
   a. That tastes terrible.
   b. You're doing that because you're jealous.

4. He's the top banana.
   a. He's very tall.
   b. He's the boss.

5. Walter got the plum job at his office!
   a. He got the best job.
   b. He got the worst job.

6. My new car is a real lemon!
   a. It's a terrible car.
   b. It's brand new and shiny.

A. TOSSED SALAD!

The letters in the following salad ingredients are all mixed up. Put the letters in their correct order to find out what's in the salad.

1. elutcet   _____lettuce_____
2. cryele   _____
3. rucemucb   _____
4. matoot   _____
5. sharid   _____

6. slionalcs   _____
7. der preepp   _____
8. chritakoe   _____
9. shurmomos   _____

B. WHICH VEGETABLE DOESN'T BELONG?

1. lettuce   cabbage   (turnip)   string bean
2. cucumber   carrot   zucchini   brussels sprout
3. mushroom   potato   tomato   turnip
4. asparagus   acorn squash   butternut squash   yam
5. green   red   kidney   pearl
6. beet   kidney   black   string
7. cabbage   lettuce   cucumber   cauliflower

C. TRUE OR FALSE?

Write **T** if the sentence is true and **F** if the sentence is false.

__T__   1. Some mushrooms can be poisonous.
____   2. Celery on the cob is very popular.
____   3. Another name for lima beans is kidney beans.
____   4. Zucchini, acorn, and butternut are all types of squash.
____   5. Pickles are made from cucumbers.
____   6. A popular dish in Latin America is black beans and rice.
____   7. Bacon, cabbage, and tomato sandwiches are very popular in the United States.
____   8. Peeling radishes can make you cry.

D. CAN YOU REMEMBER?

Without looking at the dictionary, see if you can remember . . .

3 kinds of squash.	2 kinds of peppers.	3 kinds of onions.	4 kinds of beans.
_____	_____	_____	_____
_____	_____	_____	_____
_____		_____	_____
			_____

A. CATEGORIES

Circle the word that doesn't belong. Then tell the category of each group.

Category

1. low-fat	skim	(sour)	chocolate	milk
2. chops	wings	legs	drumsticks	
3. orange	apple	halibut	pineapple	
4. oysters	paks	crabs	scallops	
5. butter	cheese	sour cream	lemonade	
6. soup	frozen dinners	tuna fish	vegetables	
7. soda	bottled water	soup	diet soda	
8. pita bread	cake	bread	rolls	
9. lamb	pork	ribs	shrimp	
10. flounder	duck	trout	tuna	
11. noodles	macaroni	scallops	spaghetti	
12. seafood	juice	beverages	milk	
13. duck	roast	turkey	chicken	
14. apple	soup	grape	tomato	

B. WHAT'S THE FOOD?

_d_	1. skim	a.	cream
___	2. cream	b.	muffins
___	3. stewing	c.	juice
___	4. juice	d.	milk
___	5. pork	e.	wings
___	6. powdered	f.	bread
___	7. ice	g.	chops
___	8. orange	h.	goods
___	9. ground	i.	foods
___	10. canned	j.	cheese
___	11. English	k.	fish
___	12. chicken	l.	water
___	13. bottled	m.	paks
___	14. pita	n.	drink
___	15. frozen	o.	meat
___	16. tuna	p.	beef

C. WHAT SHOULD I DO?

b 1. What should I do with this ice cream?

___ 2. What should I do with this frozen dinner?

___ 3. What should I do with this frozen broccoli?

___ 4. What should I do with this orange juice?

a. Defrost it and mix it with water.

b. Put it in a cone.

c. Put it in a preheated oven for 30 minutes.

d. Cook it in a saucepan with water and then drain it.

D. WHICH WORD IS CORRECT?

1. Our seafood special today is (duck (mussels)).

2. We're also having a special today on leg of (lamb   lamb chop).

3. William is a vegetarian. He doesn't eat (chicken   cheese).

4. You need to defrost these (canned vegetables   frozen vegetables).

5. We felt like having fish last night, so I made (trout   turkey).

6. My favorite pasta dish is (spaghetti   cereal).

7. How much water should I add to this (soda   powdered drink mix)?

8. When I eat (wings   chicken), I prefer to have the drumsticks.

9. (Pineapple juice   Orange juice) is usually found in the dairy section of the supermarket.

10. Many people switch to (sour cream   skim milk) when they go on a diet.

11. I'd like a sandwich on (tuna   pita), please.

A. LIKELY OR UNLIKELY?

		Likely	Unlikely
1.	Peter served olive oil as a beverage at dinner tonight.	____	✔
2.	We bought sliced provolone cheese at the deli counter.	____	____
3.	Since I only had five things, I got into the express line.	____	____
4.	I usually add flour to my coffee.	____	____
5.	There were seven shoppers working at the checkout counter.	____	____
6.	Liquid soap? It's in the beverage section over there.	____	____
7.	You'll find disposable diapers in the condiments section.	____	____
8.	You won't find herbal tea in the condiments section.	____	____
9.	I had a sandwich bag for lunch.	____	____

B. LISTENING

Listen and choose the best answer.

1. a. beef
   b. bags

2. a. nuts
   b. chips

3. a. cocoa
   b. coffee

4. a. food
   b. products

5. a. salt
   b. sauce

6. a. paper
   b. pepper

7. a. foil
   b. wrap

8. a. salad
   b. slaw

9. a. formula
   b. food

10. a. mix
    b. flour

11. a. belt
    b. cart

12. a. Foods
    b. Items

C. WORD SEARCH

Find 10 things at the supermarket that you do NOT eat.

```
S  H  O  P  P  E  R  K  E  R  N  X  F  M  O
C  T  L  A  L  U  M  I  N  U  M  F  O  I  L
A  K  O  L  A  J  G  F  M  O  N  L  D  H  B
L  E  H  T  S  P  U  R  J  T  B  X  P  L  T
E  G  D  C  T  N  D  I  A  P  E  R  S  P  Q
P  I  O  V  I  F  M  D  I  T  W  Q  T  B  N
T  A  G  A  C  C  S  P  R  F  X  C  R  I  F
I  I  F  G  W  I  P  E  S  Z  C  Z  A  A  L
C  S  O  U  R  Q  H  O  I  U  V  N  W  S  O
B  L  O  E  A  Z  N  L  Y  S  X  F  S  W  N
H  E  D  F  P  X  C  A  R  T  P  W  S  D  E
```

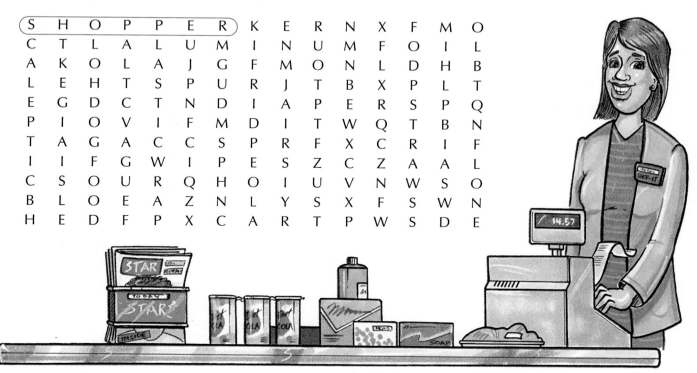

D. "BREAD AND BUTTER"

See if you can match the following popular combinations.

1. "bread and _____butter_____"

2. "macaroni and _____"

3. "oil and _____"

4. "eggs and _____"

5. "salt and _____"

6. "ketchup and _____"

E. WHICH WORD DOESN'T BELONG?

1. bologna	corned beef	(pickles)	salami
2. cheddar	American	macaroni	Swiss
3. potato	nacho	cole	corn
4. straws	formula	wipes	diapers
5. shopper	scanner	cashier	packer
6. potato	salami	seafood	macaroni
7. salt	spices	jelly	pepper
8. cups	plates	food	towels
9. coupons	candy	cashier	cash register
10. cat	baby	decaf	dog

F. ASSOCIATIONS

_f_ 1. "No dishes to wash!"

____ 2. "It's not good for your teeth!"

____ 3. "Look at the headline: ELVIS IS ALIVE!"

____ 4. "I like *Time, Newsweek,* and *Life.*"

____ 5. "That'll be $88.60."

____ 6. "Herbal is my favorite."

____ 7. "It doesn't keep me awake at night."

____ 8. "AAACHOOOOOOO!!"

____ 9. "Let's see. This weighs a pound and a half."

____ 10. "This is getting heavy to push!"

____ 11. "It's amazing! He knows exactly where to put the eggs so they don't break!"

____ 12. "It's my favorite kind of cheese."

____ 13. "I just have a few things."

____ 14. "They're great! You just throw them away!"

a. cashier

b. magazines

c. shopping cart

d. mozzarella

e. scale

f. paper plates

g. packer

h. tea

i. express checkout

j. disposable diapers

k. candy

l. tabloid

m. tissue

n. decaf coffee

A. WHICH WORD IS CORRECT?

1. Martin, we need a (roll (bar)) of soap for the guest bathroom.
2. Susan bought a (head bunch) of grapes to add to the fruit salad.
3. Would you like a dozen (sticks ears) of corn?
4. Let's bring a (six-pack tub) of soda to the barbecue.
5. Can you please pick up a (pack roll) of gum when you go to the store?
6. The recipe calls for two (bars sticks) of butter.
7. Mary brought a (jar container) of mustard and a (tub bottle) of ketchup to the picnic.
8. We need some salad dressing. Would you buy a (pint bottle) of Russian dressing on your way home from work?
9. I'll pick up a (tube tub) of toothpaste when I go to the supermarket.
10. Jill went to the bakery to buy two (liters loaves) of French bread.
11. Kim bought three (rolls packages) of rolls and two (rolls cartons) of paper towels when she went shopping this morning.
12. Michael used a whole (carton box) of tissues when he saw the movie "Casablanca."

B. LISTENING: *WHAT ARE THEY TALKING ABOUT?*

Listen and decide what's being talked about.

1. a. coffee
   b. milk

2. a. soda
   b. jam

3. a. crackers
   b. toilet tissue

4. a. tuna fish
   b. pickles

5. a. eggs
   b. corn

6. a. lettuce
   b. green beans

7. a. ice cream
   b. butter

8. a. drink mix
   b. orange juice

9. a. toilet paper
   b. soap

C. LISTENING: *WHAT'S THE CONTAINER?*

Listen and choose the correct container or quantity.

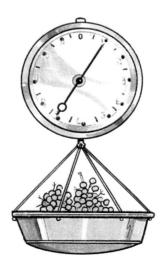

___ box	___ bunch
___ bag	___ carton
___ can	___ container
_1_ pound	___ roll

A. TRUE OR FALSE?

Write **T** if a statement is true and **F** if it is false.

T 1. There are eight ounces in a cup.

___ 2. There are three tablespoons in a teaspoon.

___ 3. A quart is bigger than a gallon.

___ 4. Two tablespoons is the same as six teaspoons.

___ 5. There are two pints in a cup.

___ 6. There are four cups in a quart.

___ 7. A gallon contains more ounces than a quart.

___ 8. A half pint holds twelve fluid ounces.

___ 9. A quarter pound hamburger contains twelve ounces of meat.

___ 10. Sixteen ozs. is the same as one lb.

___ 11. Two tsps. equal one fl. oz.

___ 12. A ten-gallon hat holds 640 fluid ounces.

B. FIGURE IT OUT!

1. Margaret's recipe calls for a pint of heavy cream, so she should put in (a cup (2 cups)).

2. Sam doesn't like food that's too spicy, so he should add only (1 tablespoon 2 teaspoons) of pepper to the chili.

3. If you want to make the sauce thicker, you should add only (1/2 cup 8 ounces) of milk.

4. Scott wants to make fruit punch. The recipe says to use a gallon of juice to serve eight people. Since there will be only four people at lunch, he needs to cut the recipe in half and add only (1 pint 2 quarts) of juice.

5. Barbara is trying to figure out how much spaghetti to cook for six people. The directions on the box say that sixteen ounces will make eight servings. Barbara wants to be sure her guests can have second helpings, plus she'd like to bring a serving to her elderly neighbor. Barbara needs to buy (1 pound 2 pounds) of spaghetti.

6. The recipe says I need four ounces of cheese and eight ounces of meat, so I guess I should buy (1/3 lb. 1/4 lb.) of provolone and (3/4 lb. 1/2 lb.) of ham at the supermarket.

A. HELP!

Match the most appropriate answer on the right with the question on the left.

_d_ 1. What should I do with the turkey?   a. Boil it!

___ 2. What should I do with this banana?   b. Steam it!

___ 3. What should I do with this water?   c. Fill it with water!

___ 4. What should I do with this bread?   d. Carve it!

___ 5. What should I do with this broccoli?   e. Microwave it!

___ 6. What should I do with this cheese?   f. Peel it!

___ 7. What should I do with this pot?   g. Slice it!

___ 8. This muffin is frozen. What should I do with it?   h. Grate it!

B. LISTENING: *WHAT ARE THEY TALKING ABOUT?*

Listen and decide what's being talked about.

1. a. bananas
   b. cranberries

2. a. pudding
   b. steak

3. a. flour
   b. rice

4. a. salt
   b. onion

5. a. eggs
   b. tomatoes

6. a. hamburgers
   b. potatoes

C. LISTENING: *WHAT'S THE CATEGORY?*

Listen and choose the appropriate category.

| ___ Foods that are carved. | _1_ Foods that are poured. | ___ Foods that are grated. |
| ___ Foods that are chopped. | ___ Foods that are baked. | ___ Foods that are grilled. |

A. WHAT'S THE FOOD?

a. chili	**d.** muffin	**g.** pizza	**j.** danish
b. 7-Up	**e.** hamburger	**h.** bagel	**k.** submarine
c. lemonade	**f.** pita	**i.** kinds of bread	**l.** fried chicken

_g_ 1. It's made with tomato sauce, and we often order this by the slice.

____ 2. Beef served in a roll or bun.

____ 3. This roll is the name of an underwater vehicle.

____ 4. This is a refreshing natural summer drink.

____ 5. This has a hole in the middle and is often toasted.

____ 6. This is often called pocket bread because of its shape.

____ 7. This sweet breakfast treat has jam or cheese on it.

____ 8. This is served in a bowl and is usually spicy.

____ 9. Pumpernickel, whole wheat, and rye.

____ 10. A typical one is blueberry or bran.

____ 11. An order usually contains two or three pieces, and it often tastes greasy.

____ 12. This is not a cola drink.

B. WHAT'S FOR BREAKFAST?

Circle the foods below that you think North Americans typically might have for breakfast.

hot dog	(donut)	bowl of chili	iced tea	taco	danish	slice of pizza
lemonade	bagel	coffee	croissant	egg salad sandwich		submarine roll
	muffin	hamburger	biscuit			

C. LISTENING: *WHAT FOOD ARE THEY TALKING ABOUT?*

Listen and decide what food is being talked about.

1. **a.** taco
   b. pizza

2. **a.** lemonade
   b. coffee

3. **a.** Diet Coke
   b. 7-Up

4. **a.** iced tea
   b. fried chicken

5. **a.** chicken salad sandwich
   b. roast beef sandwich

6. **a.** chili
   b. croissant

A. AT THE RIVERSIDE RESTAURANT

Put the following conversation in the correct order.

____ I'll have the Greek salad.

____ Would you like coffee and dessert?

____ Yes, I'd like the shrimp cocktail.

____ Could I have the check, please?

_1_ Would you care for an appetizer?

____ I'll have the meatloaf, mashed potatoes, and a salad.

____ Here's your bill. Thank you.

____ I'll have the apple pie with ice cream, please.

____ Are you ready to order your main course?

____ What kind of salad would you like?

B. FOOD TALK!

Check your understanding of the following ways of describing food. Then choose the correct word in the sentences below.

burnt	overcooked	tasty
cold	raw	undercooked
crisp	salty	warm
delicious	sour	watery
fresh	spicy	wilted
hard	stale	wonderful
out of this world	sweet	

1. He loved the meatloaf. It was (sour (tasty)).
2. (Crisp   Wilted) lettuce is the best kind to use in a salad.
3. He enjoyed the french fries because they (were   weren't) too salty.
4. All my guests loved the mixed vegetables. They thought they were (out of this world   watery).
5. Everybody liked the (fresh   stale) bread.
6. Overcooked fish is (never   usually) raw.
7. Hard potatoes (are   aren't) very tender.
8. Sally likes (spicy   sweet) coffee. That's why she adds a lot of sugar.
9. The noodles had been cooked too long and were (soggy   undercooked).
10. He forgot to turn on the stove and the veal cutlets were completely (burnt   raw).
11. These carrots aren't overcooked at all. They're (terrible   wonderful)!
12. He cut the beef right after taking it out of the oven, while it was still (cold   warm).

A. COLOR ASSOCIATIONS

What colors describe the following objects?

1. a lemon _____yellow_____
2. a tomato _____
3. snow _____
4. an olive _____
5. a lime _____

6. the sky _____
7. a cherry _____
8. a canary _____
9. eggplant _____
10. an orange _____

B. MIXING COLORS

1. If you mix red and white, you get _____pink_____.
2. If you mix red and yellow, you get _____.
3. If you mix blue and yellow, you get _____.
4. If you mix red and blue, you get _____.
5. If you mix black and white, you get _____.
6. If you mix red and green, you get _____.

C. COLORFUL EXPRESSIONS!

| red | pink | orange | yellow | green | blue | purple | black | white | gray | brown |

1. Did you see him blush? He turned bright _____red_____.
2. I'm sad. I'm feeling kind of _____ today.
3. It's a very cloudy day. Everything looks so _____ and drab.
4. Jack got into a fight today. His eye is completely _____ and blue.
5. Evelyn is _____ with envy over the neighbors' new swimming pool.
6. I was so cold, my faced started to turn _____.
7. Do you know George Gershwin's "Rhapsody in _____?"
8. When someone is afraid to do something, we say that person is _____.
9. Look at that _____ flag! That means they're surrendering!
10. In the U.S. people often wear _____ to a funeral.
11. His shirt was hot _____, and his pants were neon _____. What a terrible combination!
12. Don't shoot 'til you see the _____s of their eyes!
13. You must stop when you see a _____ school bus with its lights flashing.
14. When Timmy thought there was a burglar in the house, he turned _____ as a ghost.

A. WHO WEARS WHAT?

Decide whether the following clothing is typically worn by women (W), by men (M), or by both (B).

1. blouse   <u>W</u>
2. shirt   ___
3. uniform   ___
4. tuxedo   ___
5. slacks   ___

6. suit   ___
7. shorts   ___
8. gown   ___
9. skirt   ___
10. tie   ___

11. three-piece suit   ___
12. sports jacket   ___
13. cardigan   ___
14. bowtie   ___
15. jumpsuit   ___

B. WHAT TO WEAR?

Decide which of the following articles of clothing might be appropriate to wear to the activities below. There may be more than one answer.

a. flannel shirt	**i.** dress shirt
b. shorts	**j.** necktie
c. blouse	**k.** overalls
d. tuxedo	**l.** gown
e. three-piece suit	**m.** suit
f. uniform	**n.** dress
g. jeans	**o.** skirt
h. bowtie	**p.** jersey

1. John is going to a very formal party.   <u>d, h, i</u>
2. Janet is going to play tennis with her friend.   _____
3. Bob is going to work. He's a nurse.   _____
4. Mr. Jensen is going to a job interview.   _____
5. Mrs. Jensen is going to a job interview, too.   _____
6. Ms. Wilson is going to a very elegant wedding.   _____
7. Roger is going to work in his yard. The weather is cool today.   _____

C. LISTENING

Listen and choose the best answer.

1. a. polo shirt
   b. cardigan *(circled)*
2. a. blouse
   b. suit
3. a. sport shirt
   b. dress shirt

4. a. sweater
   b. turtleneck
5. a. corduroys
   b. evening gown
6. a. flannel shirt
   b. short-sleeved shirt

A. WHAT KIND OF SHOES DO THEY NEED?

Decide which shoes would be most appropriate for the following people and situations. There may be more than one possible answer.

a. flip-flops	**d.** high tops	**g.** sandals	**j.** high heels
b. running shoes	**e.** moccasins	**h.** hiking boots	**k.** sneakers
c. cowboy boots	**f.** boots	**i.** work boots	**l.** pumps

1.   Bob and Sara are going to the beach today. _____ *a, g* _____
2.   I'm going to jog this morning. _____
3.   Barbara is going to a job interview today. _____
4.   It's snowing, and Dave has to go to the bank. _____
5.   The Smith family is going mountain climbing. _____
6.   Bill is going to play basketball this morning. _____
7.   Susan is going to a formal party this evening. _____
8.   I just got a part in a Hollywood western movie! _____

B. LISTENING: *WHAT'S BEING DESCRIBED?*

Listen and decide what's being described.

___ slippers	___ boxer shorts
___ long johns	_1_ pajamas
___ bathrobe	___ undershirt

C. LISTENING

Listen and choose the best answer.

1. **a.** loafers
   b. running shoes *(circled)*

2. **a.** pumps
   b. high tops

3. **a.** pajamas
   b. nightgowns

4. **a.** half-slip
   b. tee shirt

5. **a.** moccasins
   b. sneakers

6. **a.** stockings
   b. underpants

7. **a.** heels
   b. hiking boots

8. **a.** thongs
   b. boots

9. **a.** athletic supporters
   b. pumps

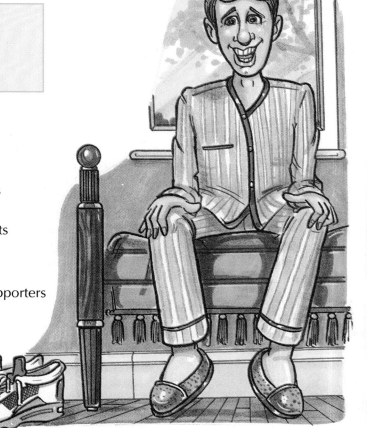

A. WHICH WORD DOESN'T BELONG?

1. poncho (overcoat) trenchcoat rubbers
2. tank top beret cap sweatband
3. running tennis lycra sweat
4. jacket hat scarf mask
5. windbreaker leotard sweatband tights

B. WHICH WOULDN'T YOU WEAR?

Decide which of the following clothing items you probably WOULDN'T wear in these situations.

1. . . . to go skiing.

   parka
   ski jacket
   (trenchcoat)
   (rubbers)
   ear muffs
   scarf
   (leotard)

2. . . . to walk to the bus on a rainy day.

   poncho
   rubbers
   trenchcoat
   lycra shorts
   raincoat

3. . . . to go jogging on a chilly morning.

   sweatshirt
   down vest
   tee shirt
   overcoat
   tank top
   windbreaker

4. . . . to go jogging on a hot summer day.

   tee shirt
   rubbers
   ski mask
   tank top
   baseball cap
   sweatband

5. . . . to work out at a health club.

   bomber jacket
   tights
   sweatband
   down jacket
   leotard
   scarf
   tank top

6. . . . to go to a ballet class.

   ear muffs
   rain hat
   beret
   leotard
   mittens
   tights
   sweatband

C. A LETTER FROM SEATTLE

gloves	vest	windbreaker	mittens	hat
scarf	rubbers	raincoat	jacket	earmuffs

Dear Mom,

How is everything back home in Mexico? Classes are going well, and I'm ready for the cold weather here in Seattle. I went shopping for a coat the other day and ended up with much more!

I told the salesperson I needed a coat, and she asked me what kind. "Do you have a _____raincoat_____ [1]? It rains a lot in this area. You should also buy a pair of _____ [2] to keep your shoes dry on rainy days. And remember! It can get cool in the fall. A _____ [3] will protect you from the wind. You'll need some type of winter coat. A down _____ [4] or _____ [5] is good because it will really keep you warm. You'll also need _____ [6] or _____ [7] to keep your hands from freezing. Of course, a _____ [8] is nice to have around your neck as well. For your head, you'll want a _____ [9] and maybe even some _____ [10] for your ears."

Mom, she had me so worried about the weather here that I bought everything! But don't worry. I'm taking care of myself, and I'll be nice and warm this winter!

Love
José

A. CAN YOU FIND . . .?

Look through the list of words on page 60 of the Picture Dictionary and see if you can find . . .

4 items that go around your neck.

beads

_____

_____

_____

6 items that can be used to carry things.

_____

_____

_____

_____

_____

_____

4 accessories usually worn with shirts, pants, and ties.

_____

_____

_____

_____

2 pieces of jewelry that can be worn on the wrist.

_____

_____

B. LIKELY OR UNLIKELY?

		Likely	Unlikely
1.	When Roger and Sally got married, they exchanged wedding bands.	✔	___
2.	Michael fastened his tie with his belt.	___	___
3.	Irene wore a lovely backpack around her neck.	___	___
4.	Nancy wore a beautiful bracelet on her right shoulder and a watch on her left.	___	___
5.	Marvin carries his important papers in his briefcase.	___	___
6.	Francine looked lovely! She wore a beautiful pearl pin on her wrist.	___	___
7.	Don't forget your umbrella! The weather forecast is for showers.	___	___
8.	I always carry extra money with me in my wallet.	___	___
9.	My sister wants something with a longer strap than a pocketbook, so I bought her a change purse.	___	___
10.	Richard keeps his credit cards in a tote bag that he carries in his right pocket.	___	___
11.	Carol wears a beautiful gold key ring on the fourth finger of her left hand.	___	___

C. LISTENING: *WHAT IS IT?*

Listen and decide what's being described.

___ briefcase	___ belt	___ engagement ring	_1_ purse
___ pearls	___ backpack	___ book bag	___ wedding ring

A. WHAT'S THE WORD?

1. **A.** I need to shorten the sleeves on this jacket.
   B. You do. They're so (short (long)), they're almost in your coffee cup!

2. **A.** You know, Carol, I think they'll be uncomfortable to wear to work.
   B. I agree. I think I'll buy the ones with the (higher   lower) heels.

3. **A.** In my opinion, the design is much too plain.
   B. Absolutely! I think the (solid   print) one will be better.

4. **A.** I've gained so much weight I'll never be able to wear those new pants I bought last spring.
   B. It's too bad you didn't buy a (tighter   looser) pair.

5. **A.** I'm not sure you'll be able to wear that coat during the wintertime. It can get extremely cold here in January and February.
   B. Hmm. I guess I should consider buying a (lighter   heavier) coat.

6. **A.** I don't like the striped one. It's too wide.
   B. I don't like it either. Let's find a (wider   narrower) one.

B. LISTENING: *THE FASHION SHOW*

Match the description you hear with the appropriate design.

C. LISTENING: *WEDDING GOSSIP*

Listen and complete each nasty sentence of this couple gossiping at a family wedding.

1. Agnes   (a.) plain   b. fancy
2. Cousin Millie   a. high   b. low
3. Uncle Wally   a. loose   b. tight
4. Aunt Esther   a. long   b. short
5. Louise   a. heavy   b. light
6. Ellie   a. narrow   b. wide
7. Uncle Jake   a. dark   b. light

A. GOING SHOPPING

In which department would you find the following?

1. a sportcoat   <u>Men's Clothing</u>
2. a pearl necklace   _____
3. a personal computer   _____
4. a child's snowsuit   _____

5. a king-size bed   _____
6. saucepans   _____
7. an evening gown   _____
8. a refrigerator   _____

9. a bottle of French cologne   _____

B. LISTENING: *ATTENTION SHOPPERS!*

Match the following announcements to the appropriate department.

___ Furniture Department	___ Women's Clothing	___ Men's Clothing
___ Household Appliances	___ Perfume Counter	___ Housewares
_1_ Children's Clothing	___ Electronics Department	___ Jewelry Counter

C. HELP ME!

What are the *department store solutions* to the problems below?

a. water fountain	**d.** Gift Wrap Counter
b. snack bar	**e.** store directory
c. Customer Service Counter	**f.** elevator

_d_ 1. "I need my purchase wrapped."

___ 2. "I don't know where the departments are located."

___ 3. "I'm really thirsty!"

___ 4. "I'm hungry."

___ 5. "I want to get a store credit card."

___ 6. "My grandmother is in a wheelchair and can't climb stairs."

D. LISTENING: *WHERE ARE THEY?*

Listen and decide in which departments or areas of a department store you would most likely hear the following conversations.

___ Customer Service Counter	_1_ Housewares	___ escalator
___ snack bar	___ elevator	___ Gift Wrap Counter
___ parking garage	___ Children's Clothing	___ Women's Clothing

A. WHAT AM I?

alarm clock	camcorder	set of headphones	speaker	VCR
blank videotape	record player	shortwave radio	TV	Walkman

Some say I'm old-fashioned, even obsolete. But for playing your records I can't be beat!

1. _____record player_____

Take me anywhere to record sights and sounds. I'm a handy gadget to have around!

2. _____

There's nothing on me when I come home from the store. But fill me up with programs galore!

3. _____

Just put me on from ear to ear for beautiful music you want to hear!

4. _____

In glorious color or black-and-white, I bring you the world all day and all night!

5. _____

You rent a movie and want to play it. I'll do that and more—tape a program and save it!

6. _____

I sit on the floor, just looking around. But out of me comes the most incredible sound!

7. _____

Wherever you go just take me along. I'm easy to carry, and I'll play you a song!

8. _____

I'll get you up whenever you wish. Just set me correctly, just push the right switch!

9. _____

If you buy a good one whose reception is strong, you'll hear London or Paris or even Hong Kong!

10. _____

B. LISTENING: A SALE AT TECH HI-FI

Listen to the commercial and fill in the correct information.

1. Sony 8" TV: ____20____ % off
2. VCR: _____% off
3. videotapes: 4 for $_____
4. CD players: _____ to _____ % off
5. Walkman: up to _____ % off
6. shortwave: as low as $_____

A. CROSSWORD PUZZLE

ACROSS

3. An accountant needs this.

4. If there isn't enough light to take a picture, you can use this.

8. This sends copies by phone.

9. You show slides and movies on this.

10. This makes distant objects appear closer.

14. This is a computer you can travel with.

16. This is a *three-legged* stand for a camera.

DOWN

1. This prints what you have typed.

2. You type on this.

5. This transmits computer information via phone lines.

6. This helps you figure out complicated math.

7. You need this for your camera to take photographs.

11. You move and click this when you use your computer.

12. This shows what you're typing on your computer.

13. The disk goes here.

15. This lets you adapt electronic equipment to a different voltage.

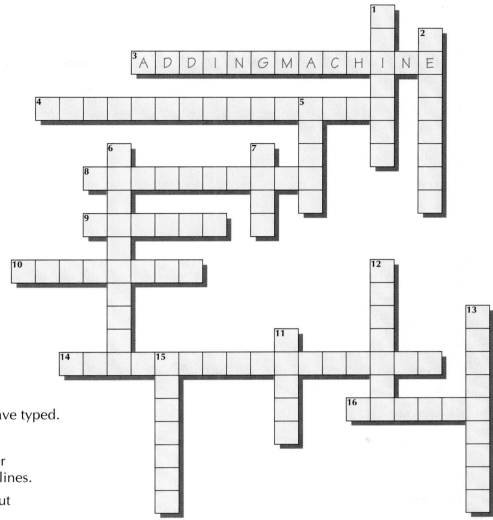

ADDINGMACHINE

B. LISTENING

Listen and choose the best answer.

1. **a.** zoom lens
   b. fax machine

2. a. adapters
   b. answering machines

3. a. software
   b. tripods

4. a. cameras
   b. typewriters

5. a. camera case
   b. portable phone

6. a. slide projector
   b. modem

7. a. flash attachment
   b. monitor

8. a. printer
   b. calculator

9. a. disk drive
   b. keyboard

THE TOY STORE

A. WHICH TOY DOESN'T BELONG?

1. train set   (bicycle)   racing car set   matchbox car
2. wading pool   doll house   bicycle   swing set
3. coloring book   paint set   markers   crayons
4. action figure   toy truck   doll   stuffed animal
5. trading cards   hula hoop   beach ball   rubber ball
6. wagon   skateboard   swing set   tricycle

B. A LETTER TO SANTA

Dear Santa,

I have a big list this year because I'm writing for my brother and sister as well as myself. First of all, my dolls need a place to live. Could you give me a _____doll house_____ [1]? It would be nice if I could also have _____ [2] to go in it. Do you know that _____ [3]s are very popular? In case you don't know, they're plastic rings that you swing around your hips or waist. I think this would be a good present for my little sister, who always wants to play with mine. She also hates taking baths. I thought some _____ [4] instead of regular soap would make the tub more fun for her. My little brother would like a _____ [5] so that he and his friends can pretend they're police officers and talk to each other from a distance. He also likes science, so a _____ [6] might be a good idea for him. Also, we'll be spending a lot of time at the beach next summer. Could you send a _____ [7] and a _____ [8] to play with in the sand? A _____ [9] would also be a good thing to throw around the beach as well. I love to paint and draw, so _____ [10], _____ [11], and a _____ [12] would also be very nice presents. Thanks, Santa.

Love,
Virginia

A. LISTENING

Listen and write the amount of money you hear.

1. _____$19.50_____
2. _____
3. _____
4. _____
5. _____
6. _____
7. _____
8. _____
9. _____

B. HOW MUCH DO THEY COST?

Match the following items with the appropriate prices.

_c_ 1. a hamburger and a coke   a. $90,000

___ 2. a car   b. $9,500

___ 3. a new house   c. $2.50

___ 4. a piece of candy   d. $85.00

___ 5. a camera   e. $20.00

___ 6. a pair of gloves   f. 7¢

C. ANOTHER WAY OF SAYING IT

Replace the underlined amounts of money with other ways of saying them.

1. A telephone call costs a dime.   _____ten cents_____

2. Bobby lost a nickel.   _____

3. "Find a penny, pick it up. All day long you'll have good luck!"   _____

What do you think these mean?

4. Can you lend me a buck?   _____

5. If I had a few grand, I'd buy a car.   _____

D. GETTING CHANGE

What change will you receive if you give a cashier . . .

1. a $5 bill for $3.85 in groceries?   _____$1.15_____

2. a $20 bill for $14 of gasoline?   _____

3. a $1 bill for a 75¢ box of candy?   _____

4. a quarter for a 20¢ newspaper?   _____

5. $40 for a $30 dinner?   _____

6. two dollars for four 29¢ stamps?   _____

A. BANK TALK

application	book	card	order	register	slip	statement

1. You need to fill out this deposit _____ *slip* _____ .
2. It's so convenient to use the ATM _____ .
3. I need to send a money _____ .
4. I just received my monthly _____ .
5. Here's my loan _____ .
6. Where's my bank _____ ?
7. I record all my transactions in my check _____ .

B. LIKELY OR UNLIKELY?

	Likely	Unlikely
1. George needed to take money out of the bank, so he filled out a deposit slip.	___	✔
2. Margaret charged a new sofa on her credit card.	___	___
3. You don't always have to fill out a loan application. If a bank officer knows you need the money, all you have to do is fill out a withdrawal slip.	___	___
4. I keep a record in my check register of all the checks I've written.	___	___
5. Most people keep their monthly statement in a safe deposit box at the bank.	___	___
6. At my bank, automatic tellers are bank employees who help customers with their banking business.	___	___

C. LISTENING: *THE BANK ROBBERY*

Listen and decide whether the following statements are true (T) or false (F).

_T_ 1. The robber demanded that the teller open the vault.

___ 2. The teller didn't have the combination.

___ 3. The bank officer told the robber to put one million dollars into a safe deposit box.

___ 4. Luckily, a security guard was in the lobby and set off one of the ATM machines.

___ 5. The robber was stopped by the police.

A. WHICH WORD DOESN'T BELONG?

1. sideburn   (eyelid)   eyebrow   mustache
2. chin   shin   thigh   buttocks
3. pinky   wrist   index   ring
4. heel   toe   knuckle   ankle
5. temple   iris   pupil   cornea
6. large intestine   bladder   liver   lip
7. veins   lungs   pancreas   kidneys
8. palm   thumb   calf   knuckle

B. WHICH WORD IS CORRECT?

1. A. Did you hurt your whole foot?
   B. No. Just my ((ankle)   palm).

2. A. Alan broke his (thigh   jaw).
   B. I know. He won't be able to eat for several weeks.

3. A. Has your diet been successful?
   B. Yes. I've already taken two inches off my (wrist   waist).

4. A. Did the doctor check your eye?
   B. Yes. She thinks my (cornea   nostril) is damaged.

5. A. Is the pain in your temple?
   B. Actually, my whole (foot   forehead) hurts.

6. A. Were those boxes heavy?
   B. I almost broke my (back   brain) carrying them!

7. A. Was your husband's (stomach   lung) surgery successful?
   B. Yes. His digestion has improved a lot since the operation.

8. A. What happened to your hand?
   B. I sprained my (iris   pinky).

9. A. My (leg   nose) is running!
   B. Here's a handkerchief.

10. A. Mr. Jones, I think you're going to need open (heart   head) surgery.
    B. Oh, no!

11. A. Which part of your leg did you injure?
    B. My (chin   shin).

12. A. How did your son break his (sideburn   shoulder)?
    B. Playing squash.

13. A. Please turn and face me so I can examine your (back   abdomen).
    B. Okay.

14. A. Mrs. Blackwell, I'm going to have to remove your (gall bladder   bones).
    B. I'm sure I'll feel better after the operation.

15. A. Which part of your (arm   armpit) did you sprain?
    B. My elbow.

C. WHAT'S THE ACTION?

Match the action with the correct part of the body.

a. arm	**f.** fingernail	**k.** knuckle	**p.** stomach
b. brain	**g.** hair	**l.** leg	**q.** teeth
c. earlobe	**h.** heart	**m.** lips	**r.** throat
d. eye	**i.** index finger	**n.** lungs	**s.** toe
e. eyelid	**j.** knee	**o.** nostril	

_d_ **1.** see

___ **2.** chew

___ **3.** breathe

___ **4.** bend

___ **5.** throw

___ **6.** smell

___ **7.** think

___ **8.** run

___ **9.** comb

___ **10.** swallow

___ **11.** digest

___ **12.** point

___ **13.** blink

___ **14.** kiss

___ **15.** pump

___ **16.** pierce

___ **17.** crack

___ **18.** file

___ **19.** stub

D. "PUT YOUR BEST FOOT FORWARD!"

See if you can figure out which parts of the body are used in the following expressions. Some words may be used more than once.

1. Try hard and "put your best _____foot_____ forward"!

2. Don't say anything. Just "hold your _____"!

3. Let's discuss this in person, "_____ to _____."

4. I think I'll "_____ around" to find out what's happening.

5. They danced together "_____ to _____."

6. Be brave and "keep your _____ up"!

7. You'll feel better if you "get that off your _____" and talk about it.

8. He "_____ed his way" into the crowd.

9. Uncle George is generous. He "has a big _____."

10. Stop bothering me! Just "get off my _____"!

11. My son has gotten so thin he's just "_____ and _____s"!

12. Another way of saying "hitchhike" is to "_____ a ride."

13. The race was very close. They ran "_____ and _____."

14. The president has to "_____ a lot of responsibilities."

15. I'm so upset with Alan's behavior. I don't think I can "_____ it" much longer.

16. In the theater, it is considered good luck before a performance to tell an actor or actress to "break a _____."

back
bone
cheek
chest
chin
face
elbow
foot
heart
leg
neck
nose
shoulder
skin
stomach
thumb
tongue

A. WHAT'S AILING THEM?

1. I hear a ringing sound!

   (a.) He has an earache.
   b. He has a sore throat.

2. My dentist is very concerned.

   a. She has the hiccups.
   b. She has a toothache.

3. I can't breathe at all!

   a. No wonder! You're exhausted
   b. No wonder! You're congested.

4. My head is spinning!

   a. He's swollen.
   b. He feels faint.

5. My doctor says I shouldn't lift anything.

   a. She has a backache.
   b. She has an earache.

6. I can't talk!

   a. He has diarrhea.
   b. He has laryngitis.

7. I'm having trouble swallowing!

   a. I'm not surprised. You have a bad sore throat.
   b. That's because you're scratching.

8. Believe it or not, it's over 102 degrees!

   a. He's bloated.
   b. He has a fever.

9. Quick! I need a bandaid!

   a. She cut herself, and she's bleeding.
   b. She's itchy, and she's sneezing.

10. It's all over my body!

    a. He has a cold.
    b. He has a rash.

11. You ought to see how red my back is! I'll never sit at the beach all day again!

    a. She has a sunburn.
    b. She has a backache.

B. ABSOLUTELY MISERABLE!

I feel terrible! I was ((hurt) exhausted)[1] in a car accident the other day. I sprained my (nose   wrist)[2], twisted my (knuckle   ankle)[3], and dislocated my (knee   iris)[4]. Also, I scraped my (cornea   veins)[5] and bruised my right (hip   sideburn)[6]. On top of that, this morning I came down with a terrible (wart   virus)[7]. My head is (exhausted   congested)[8], my stomach is (bloated   dizzy)[9], and I have a stiff (lip   neck)[10]. I feel absolutely miserable! I hope I get better soon.

C. OH, MY ACHING BACK!

See if you can figure out how we describe the following ailments.

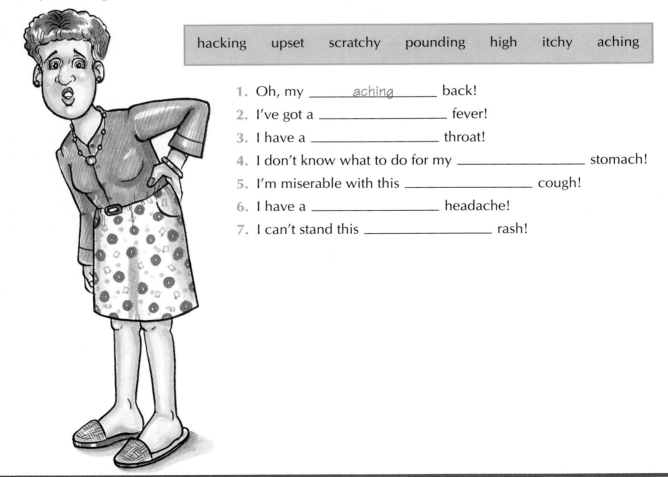

hacking	upset	scratchy	pounding	high	itchy	aching

1. Oh, my _____aching_____ back!
2. I've got a _____ fever!
3. I have a _____ throat!
4. I don't know what to do for my _____ stomach!
5. I'm miserable with this _____ cough!
6. I have a _____ headache!
7. I can't stand this _____ rash!

A. WHAT'S THE WORD?

cardiologist	needle	pediatrician	stethoscope
dentist	obstetrician	psychiatrist	surgeon
examination table	optometrist	scale	thermometer

1. I'm having problems with my eyes. I really need to see a good _____optometrist_____.

2. I'm going to see my _____. I have a painful cavity.

3. My husband has been having chest pains. He needs to see a _____ right away.

4. All our friends take their children to Dr. Peters. She's an excellent _____.

5. All the mothers-to-be like Dr. Williams. They think he's a wonderful _____.

6. All right, Mr. Taylor. Come into my office and stand on the _____ so I can weigh you. Then sit on the _____ _____ and I'll listen to your heart with this _____.

7. I recommend Dr. Davis. He's a well-known _____ who specializes in treating depression.

8. What's the name of the _____ who took out your appendix?

9.

Don't be afraid, Timmy. I'm just going to take your temperature with this _____ and give you a shot with this _____. I promise you it won't hurt.

B. LISTENING: *WHERE ARE THEY?*

Listen and decide where these people are.

____ in the emergency room
____ in the X-ray room
____ in a psychiatrist's office
_1_ in the examination room
____ in the optometrist's office
____ in the operating room
____ in an ambulance
____ at the dentist's office

MEDICAL TREATMENT AND THE HOSPITAL

A. A GOOD IDEA!/NOT A GOOD IDEA!

Decide whether or not the following treatments would be appropriate.

	A Good Idea	Not a Good Idea
1. You should put a bandaid on that cut.	✔	___
2. Rest in bed for a few days, drink fluids, and I'm sure your cold will be better soon.	___	___
3. Gargling is good if you're in a cast.	___	___
4. I recommend surgery to take care of your virus.	___	___
5. I'll give you an injection with this thermometer.	___	___
6. This is a bad cut. I think you need stitches.	___	___
7. Your ankle is broken. We'll need to put a cast on it.	___	___
8. I recommend physical therapy. That should help the psychological problems you're having.	___	___
9. Tim is thirty pounds overweight. His doctor told him to exercise and go on a diet.	___	___
10. When Carla broke her leg, the doctor told her she needed a sling.	___	___
11. After Bob stepped on a rusty nail, his doctor gave him a tetanus shot and a prescription for Vitamin C.	___	___
12. I was feeling weak and tired last month. My doctor thought my blood might be low in iron, so he recommended X-rays and counseling.	___	___

B. LISTENING: *WHAT ARE THEY TALKING ABOUT?*

Listen and decide what's being talked about.

___ surgery   ___ X-rays

___ stitches   ___ a hospital gown

___ gargling   ___ the call button

___ an I.V.   _1_ exercise

___ a medical chart ___ the bed pan

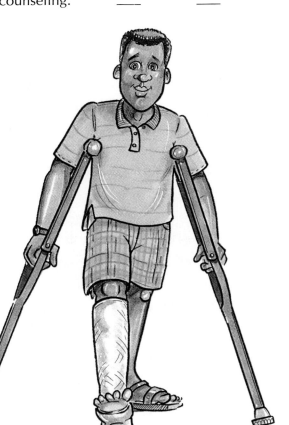

C. ASSOCIATIONS

_d_ 1. diet   a. legs

___ 2. gargle   b. cut

___ 3. prescription c. drip

___ 4. sling   d. weight

___ 5. bandaid   e. therapist

___ 6. crutches   f. drug

___ 7. I.V.   g. throat

___ 8. counseling   h. arm

76

A. AILMENTS AND REMEDIES

You're a doctor working in a busy health clinic. Today you're seeing a lot of patients. What will you suggest for the following ailments?

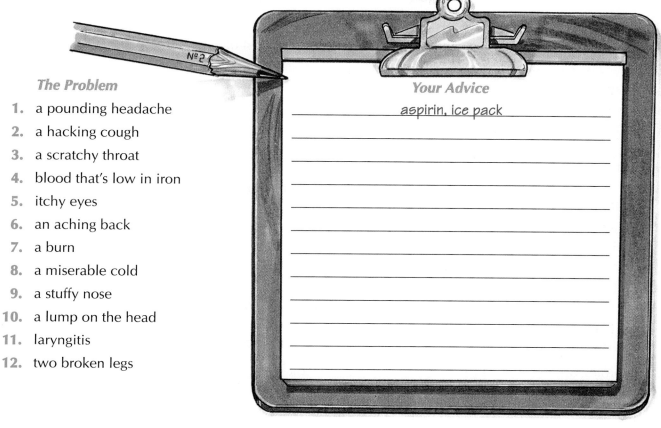

The Problem

1. a pounding headache
2. a hacking cough
3. a scratchy throat
4. blood that's low in iron
5. itchy eyes
6. an aching back
7. a burn
8. a miserable cold
9. a stuffy nose
10. a lump on the head
11. laryngitis
12. two broken legs

Your Advice

aspirin, ice pack

B. INTERNAL OR EXTERNAL?

Decide how the following are taken—internally (**I**) or externally (**E**)?

___I___ 1. aspirin   ____ 4. throat lozenges   ____ 7. cold tablets

____ 2. cough syrup   ____ 5. lotion   ____ 8. ice pack

____ 3. ointment   ____ 6. antacid tablets   ____ 9. vitamins

C. *TAKE* OR *USE*?

1. Go home, stay in bed, and ((take) use) two aspirin.
2. For a backache, I always (take use) a heating pad.
3. Jack needs to (take use) decongestant spray.
4. Barbara's doctor told her to (take use) eye drops twice a day.
5. When Carol was pregnant, she (took used) vitamins.
6. After Steve won the pie-eating contest, he needed to (take use) antacid tablets.

A. WHICH WORD IS CORRECT?

1. You forgot to put the (book of stamps (zip code)) on the envelope.

2. Please drop this (letter postman) in the mail slot.

3. I just received a (parcel letter) from my cousin Bertha. I hope everything is okay.

4. Please get a (money order mailbox) when you're at the post office.

5. Henry is moving to a new condo next month. He needs to fill out a
   (return address change-of-address) form.

6. Excuse me, sir. This (window mailbox) is closed. Please go to the other one and somebody
   will help you.

7. Send this package the fastest way possible. It needs to get there overnight. Send it
   (first class express mail).

8. Margaret wants to make sure that her landlord receives her letter. She should send it
   (registered first class).

9. Oh, no! I forgot to put my (return address postmark) on the package I just sent to my cousin in
   Colorado. I hope it doesn't get lost!

10. Please drop these in the (mail slot mail carrier) for out-of-town mail.

11. Molly just received a beautiful (aerogramme postcard) from her niece who is in Florida.
    It has a picture of Mickey Mouse on it, and on the back it says "Wish you were here!"

12. The mail carrier's (mail bag mailbox) looks very heavy. I wonder how much mail she
    delivers every day.

13. The professor didn't need her books in a hurry, so she asked the publisher to send them
    (registered book rate).

14. Excuse me, sir. Where is this package going? The (return address address) isn't very clear.

15. Please stop at the post office and pick up a (mail bag roll of stamps).

16. Do you want to send this (aerogramme airmail) or parcel post?

17. We bought some stamps at the (stamp machine mail slot).

18. All eighteen-year-old males in the United States are required to register with the military by filling
    out a (selective service change of address) form.

19. My cousin Mark is a (postmark postal clerk) at the local post office.

B. LISTENING

Listen and choose the best answer.

1. a. mail slot
   b. window

2. a. sheet of stamps
   b. letter

3. a. mail box
   b. mail carrier

4. a. rate
   b. class

5. a. roll
   b. package

6. a. book of stamps
   b. stamp machine

A. THE MIDVILLE LIBRARY

atlas	dictionary	microfiche	reference librarian
author	encyclopedia	microfilm	reference section
call card	librarian	newspaper	shelves
call number	library assistant	periodicals section	tape
card catalog	magazine	photocopy machine	title
checkout desk	media section	record	videotape

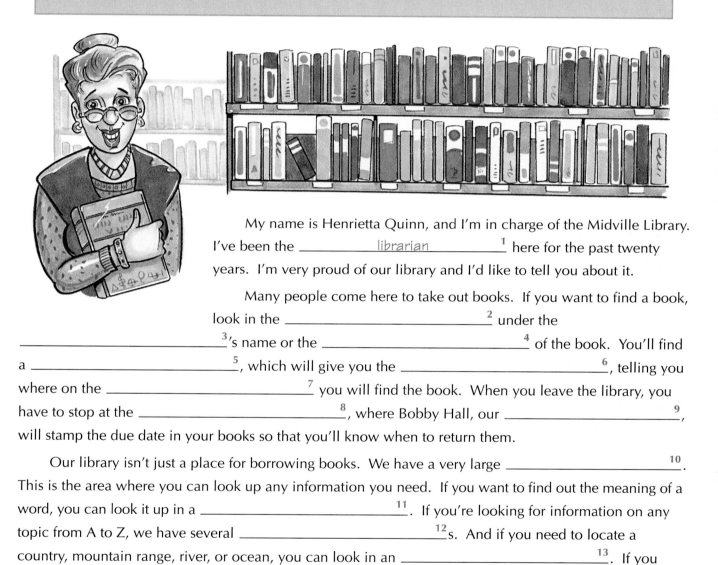

My name is Henrietta Quinn, and I'm in charge of the Midville Library. I've been the _____librarian_____ [1] here for the past twenty years. I'm very proud of our library and I'd like to tell you about it.

Many people come here to take out books. If you want to find a book, look in the _____ [2] under the _____ [3]'s name or the _____ [4] of the book. You'll find a _____ [5], which will give you the _____ [6], telling you where on the _____ [7] you will find the book. When you leave the library, you have to stop at the _____ [8], where Bobby Hall, our _____ [9], will stamp the due date in your books so that you'll know when to return them.

Our library isn't just a place for borrowing books. We have a very large _____ [10]. This is the area where you can look up any information you need. If you want to find out the meaning of a word, you can look it up in a _____ [11]. If you're looking for information on any topic from A to Z, we have several _____ [12]s. And if you need to locate a country, mountain range, river, or ocean, you can look in an _____ [13]. If you need help, Sally Barnes, our _____ [14], will be happy to assist you.

To keep up with current events both here and abroad, you can spend time in our _____ [15], where you can browse through our daily _____ [16]s and our weekly and monthly _____ [17]s. If you want to take an article home, you can make a copy on our _____ [18].

(continued)

You can also find entertainment in the library. In the _____ ¹⁹ you'll find
_____ ²⁰s and _____ ²¹s to listen to and
_____ ²²s to watch.

If you want to find an article from an old newspaper or periodical, you can look it up on the
_____ ²³ machine. Old newspapers and journals are kept on
_____ ²⁴.

So the next time you're in the neighborhood, stop by and say hello. I'd love to show you around
our library.

B. LISTENING: *WHAT ARE THEY TALKING ABOUT?*

Listen and decide what's being talked about.

___ encyclopedia	___ media section	___ dictionary
___ call card	___ checkout counter	___ atlas
___ online catalog	___ periodicals section	_1_ library card

C. LIKELY OR UNLIKELY?

	Likely	Unlikely
1. I always ask the librarian if I have any questions.	✔	___
2. When David needs to find the meaning of a word, he always looks it up in the atlas.	___	___
3. We keep our encyclopedias in the reference section over there.	___	___
4. If you're looking for a magazine, look in the media section.	___	___
5. You'll find all the books we have in our library at the checkout desk.	___	___
6. If you want to know where something is, all you have to do is ask the person at the information desk.	___	___
7. People who want to find old newspaper articles can look them up on either microfilm or microfiche.	___	___
8. All the computer diskettes in this library are on the shelves.	___	___
9. None of the call cards in our libary give the title or the author.	___	___
10. People who want to take books out of our library need a library card.	___	___
11. Ronald works as a copy machine at the Midville Library.	___	___

A. WHAT'S THE WORD?

Complete the following using words from page 77 of the Picture Dictionary.

1. The principal wants to see you in her _____ office _____.

2. All the students gathered in the school _____ for an assembly.

3. Johnny has a headache and feels warm. He should see the _____.

4. The members of the girls' marathon team run ten miles around the _____ every day.

5. My Russian _____ gives us listening and pronunciation homework that we do outside of class in the _____.

6. Sophomores who want to learn how to drive must sign up with the _____.

7. The teachers are relaxing in the _____.

8. Peggy wants to try out for the varsity basketball team. She needs to speak with the _____.

9. Lisa is having some problems at home. Her teacher is encouraging her to make an appointment to talk with the _____.

10. The principal is away at a conference. You may speak with Ms. Anderson, the _____.

11. The _____ needs to mop the floor. It's wet and slippery.

12. The members of the boys' soccer team get dressed in the _____ and then go to the _____ to warm up and practice.

B. LISTENING: *WHO'S TALKING?*

Listen and decide who is talking.

1. a. guidance counselor
   b. coach

2. a. custodian
   b. principal

3. a. principal
   b. vice-principal

4. a. driver's ed instructor
   b. coach

5. a. teacher
   b. lunchroom monitor

6. a. school nurse
   b. cafeteria worker

A. A LETTER HOME

Complete the following letter using words from pages 78-79 of the Picture Dictionary.

Dear Masako,

I've just finished my first month as an exchange student at Brookdale High. I miss you and all my friends in Tokyo, but things here are fine. I'm taking a great _____biology_____ 1 course. Last week we dissected a frog, and tomorrow we're going to dissect a worm. My _____ 2 class is also very good. I'm learning where all the countries, lakes, rivers, oceans, and mountain ranges are. I'm also discovering countries I've never even heard of! My _____ 3 course is very hard. We're reading contemporary Latin American literature. In _____ 4, I'm making a wooden table. It's a little lopsided, but I like it! I had a disaster last week in _____ 5. I burned my cake and spilled a bag of flour all over the floor!

I'm busy with a lot of extracurricular activities, too. You know how much I like to sing. Well, last week I joined the _____ 6. In the _____ 7 club, we're working on a production of *King Lear*. In addition, my class elected me to the _____ 8. Oh, one more thing. I've just submitted a few poems to the school _____ 9. I think they're going to be published in the winter issue.

That's all for now. As you can see, I'm very busy and I'm having a wonderful time. Say hello to everybody for me.

Love,
Junko

P.S. Our school _____ 10 team won the state championship last week!

B. WHICH COURSE?

Decide in which course you might hear the following.

_d_ 1. We're going to study one of Shakespeare's plays next week.

____ 2. If you think multiplication is difficult, wait until we get to long division!

____ 3. We'll practice all the letters in the middle row first.

____ 4. I'm going to write about the Roman Empire.

____ 5. Where exactly are the Himalayan mountains located?

____ 6. You're going to get to know all the rules of the road.

____ 7. We're going to talk about AIDS—how the disease is contracted and how to prevent it.

____ 8. Bonjour, class. Comment allez-vous?

____ 9. We're having a test tomorrow on atoms, neutrons, and protons.

a. typing
b. French
c. geography
d. English
e. health
f. history
g. physics
h. mathematics
i. driver's ed

C. ASSOCIATIONS

_d_ 1. soprano

____ 2. violinist

____ 3. president

____ 4. quarterback

____ 5. editor

____ 6. actor

a. student government
b. drama
c. school newspaper
d. chorus
e. football team
f. orchestra

D. LIKELY OR UNLIKELY?

	Likely	Unlikely
1. There are some excellent singers in our school choir.	✔	____
2. We learn all about cooking and nutritious eating in our industrial arts class.	____	____
3. We draw and paint in our health class.	____	____
4. Students who don't do well in math probably don't do very well in trigonometry either.	____	____
5. Geometry is a popular extracurricular activity in our school.	____	____
6. We learn the rules of the road in our driver's ed class.	____	____
7. Our school yearbook is published weekly.	____	____

E. IN MY OPINION

1. In my opinion, the most interesting subject is . . . . because . . . .

2. In my opinion, the most boring subject is . . . . because . . . .

3. I think the hardest subject is . . . . because . . . .

4. For me, the easiest subject is . . . . because . . . .

A. WHAT'S THE OCCUPATION?

accountant	barber	chef	lawyer	pharmacist	secretary
architect	butcher	gardener	mechanic	salesperson	translator
baker	carpenter	journalist	newscaster	scientist	waitress

1. Would you please give this to my _____secretary_____? He needs to fix the mistakes in this letter.

2. My sister is a famous _____. She writes for *The New York Times*.

3. I have an excellent _____ who helps with my tax returns.

4. My wife is a _____ at Lucy's Coffee Shop downtown.

5. The _____ who designed this building is very talented.

6. My son speaks seven languages. He works as a _____ at the United Nations.

7. Who is the _____ who made this fantastic bread?

8. As your _____, I think it's important for you to have a will.

9. My compliments to the _____! This was an excellent meal!

10. Ask the _____ how much of this medication you should take.

11. I'm sure some day a _____ will discover a cure for the common cold.

12. The _____ who cut your husband's hair should be fired!

13. I buy all my meat from the _____ around the corner.

14. The _____ who fixed this car didn't do a very good job. The brakes still squeak.

15. I have a part-time job as a _____ in the Children's Clothing Department.

16. I just fired our _____. All our rose bushes died!

17. We need to call a _____ to fix our broken front steps.

18. You look familiar. Aren't you the _____ on Channel 9?

B. LISTENING: *WHO'S TALKING?*

Listen and decide who is talking.

____ actor	__1__ pilot	____ taxi driver
____ cashier	____ police officer	____ teacher
____ delivery person	____ real estate agent	____ travel agent
____ farmer	____ receptionist	____ veterinarian
____ fisherman	____ stock clerk	____ waiter

C. ANALOGIES

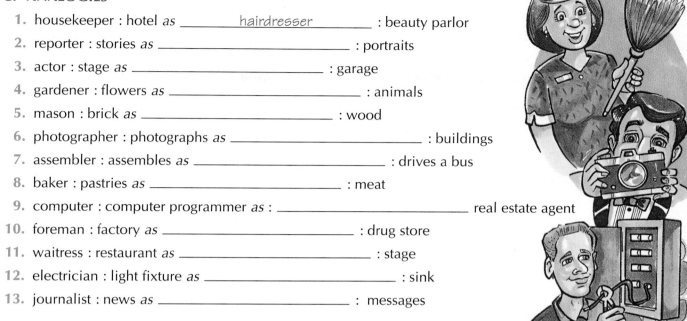

1. housekeeper : hotel *as* _____<u>hairdresser</u>_____ : beauty parlor
2. reporter : stories *as* _____ : portraits
3. actor : stage *as* _____ : garage
4. gardener : flowers *as* _____ : animals
5. mason : brick *as* _____ : wood
6. photographer : photographs *as* _____ : buildings
7. assembler : assembles *as* _____ : drives a bus
8. baker : pastries *as* _____ : meat
9. computer : computer programmer *as* : _____ real estate agent
10. foreman : factory *as* _____ : drug store
11. waitress : restaurant *as* _____ : stage
12. electrician : light fixture *as* _____ : sink
13. journalist : news *as* _____ : messages

D. LIKELY OR UNLIKELY?

		Likely	Unlikely
1.	Bob uses an architect to prepare his taxes.	___	✔
2.	The lawyer successfully defended her client.	___	___
3.	Our wedding cake was baked by an excellent carpenter.	___	___
4.	The bricks on our front walk were laid by a local mason.	___	___
5.	A famous seamstress recently discovered a cure for the flu.	___	___
6.	This office is guarded by a gardener.	___	___
7.	We called our travel agent when we decided to take a trip.	___	___
8.	Roger went to the baker up the street to get a haircut.	___	___
9.	This suit was made by a very fine tailor.	___	___
10.	When our dog is sick, we take him to a sanitation worker.	___	___
11.	The new factory was built by an excellent team of custodians.	___	___
12.	The front page story on today's paper was written by a well-known newscaster.	___	___
13.	I call an electrician when we have problems with our front light.	___	___
14.	Bertha is a housekeeper at the Plaza Hotel.	___	___
15.	We always call our local pharmacist when our sink is broken.	___	___
16.	My cousin works as a journalist at the bank.	___	___
17.	You pay the courier near the door when you leave the cafeteria.	___	___
18.	When I have a question at the library, I ask the bookkeeper.	___	___

A. WHAT'S THE ACTION?

act	clean	draw	grow	paint	serve	translate
assemble	cook	drive	guard	play	sew	type
bake	deliver	file	mow	repair	sing	wash
build	design	fly	operate	sell	teach	write

1. Do you know how to _____play_____ the guitar?

2. Here. Let me show you how to _____ this X-ray machine.

3. Mr. Jones. Please _____ these reports under the letter G.

4. I love to _____. Maybe someday I'll be in a play on Broadway.

5. I need to find someone who can _____ this letter from English into Japanese.

6. I like to _____ dishes, but I don't like to dry them afterwards.

7. We can _____ this sofa next week. What day is convenient for you?

8. I'm sorry. We don't _____ breakfast—only lunch and dinner.

9. Did you _____ this poem? It's absolutely beautiful!

10. My children know how to _____ an apple pie.

11. I think I'll _____ the walls light blue. What do you think?

12. I can't _____ a note! I have a terrible voice.

13. My daughter _____s all her papers for school on the computer. Times have certainly changed!

14. I'm a terrible artist. I can't even _____ a straight line.

15. My wife can _____ beautifully. She makes all her own clothes.

16. We _____ tomatoes and cucumbers in our backyard.

17. My husband used to _____ a bus before he retired last year.

18. Can you _____ things around the house? I can't. I'm not very handy.

19. The men who _____ the Queen's Palace in London never smile.

20. Mrs. Taylor. When are you going to _____ us the future continuous tense?

21. Ming can _____ components for circuit boards faster than anyone else in the factory.

22. We're planning to _____ a small retirement home in Florida.

23. I'm an architect. I _____ large office buildings.

24. I don't feel like _____ing dinner at home tonight. Let's go out to eat!

25. Do you want to _____ to San Francisco or should we take the train?

26. Believe it or not, Blake's Department Store is having a huge sale this week! They're _____ing everything at half-price!

27. I think I'll _____ the lawn. The grass is getting very long.

28. Susie, please _____ your room before the guests arrive!

B. WHAT DO THEY HAVE IN COMMON?

Decide what the actions below have in common.

a. Things you do to food.	**e.** Things you do in an office.
b. Things you do with your hands.	**f.** Things you do to buildings.
c. Words that rhyme.	**g.** Things you do with a vehicle.
d. Things you do to clothing.	**h.** Things you do with your voice.

1. sell
sew
wash
`d`

2. type
write
paint
`⬜`

3. bake
cook
serve
`⬜`

4. grow
sew
mow
`⬜`

5. design
construct
guard
`⬜`

6. act
teach
sing
`⬜`

7. draw
write
file
`⬜`

8. deliver
drive
fly
`⬜`

C. WHAT'S THE CATEGORY?

See if you can figure out which actions from pages 84-85 of the Picture Dictionary are associated with the following groups of words.

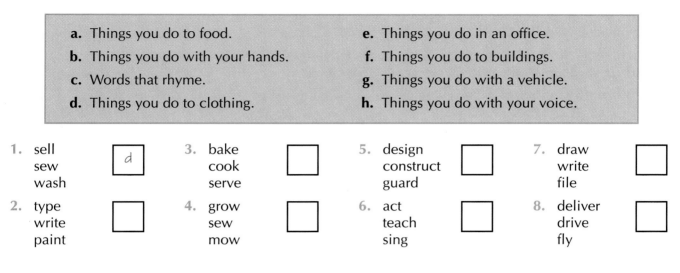

1. breakfast   lunch   dinner   Things you ___*cook*___.

2. dishes   your hands   your car   Things you _____.

3. flowers   vegetables   crops   Things you _____.

4. the guitar   soccer   games   Things you _____.

5. cakes   pies   pastries   Things you _____.

6. houses   bridges   buildings   Things you _____.

7. airplanes   kites   spaceships   Things you _____.

8. memos   letters   your name   Things you _____.

9. food   drinks   tennis balls   Things you _____.

10. English   French   typing   Things you _____.

11. trucks   cars   buses   Things you _____.

12. walls   fences   pictures   Things you _____.

13. furniture   pizzas   babies   Things you _____.

14. banks   buildings   countries' borders   Things you _____.

15. cars   appliances that don't work   things that are broken   Things you _____.

A. WHICH WORD IS CORRECT?

1. Please hang up your jacket on the (closet (coat rack)) over there.

2. There's an important meeting today with all the stockholders in the (conference room   supply room).

3. Mary has a job interview tomorrow. When she arrives, she'll probably wait in the (employee lounge   reception area) for a few minutes.

4. Let's make a fresh pot of coffee in the coffee (machine   cart).

5. Speed, accuracy, attention to detail, good spelling, and proofreading are all important skills for a (file clerk   typist).

6. The company's (boss   receptionist) usually greets people at the front desk.

7. Pens, pencils, and paper are kept in the (file cabinet   supply cabinet).

8. The (office assistant   office manager) is the person who runs the office.

9. I can barely read this. The (dry erase board   copier) must be out of ink.

10. Large boxes of past seasons' catalogs, old order forms, and outdated sales brochures are here in the (storage room   supply room).

B. LISTENING: *WHAT'S THE LAST WORD?*

Listen and complete the sentences.

___ lounge	___ closet	___ meter	___ area	___ clerk
___ station	___ cabinet	___ room	___ assistant	_1_ machine

C. LISTENING: *WHERE ARE THEY?*

Listen and decide where the conversation is taking place.

___ in the reception area

___ in the conference room

___ in the supply room

___ in the employee lounge

_1_ at the copier

___ in the mailroom

D. LISTENING: *WHO'S TALKING?*

Listen and decide who is talking.

___ boss   _1_ typist   ___ receptionist   ___ file clerk   ___ office assistant

A. WHAT'S THE WORD?

Complete the following using words from page 87 of the Picture Dictionary.

1. What a day! The _____telephone_____ didn't stop ringing, and every time I tried to transfer a call, the person got disconnected. In my opinion, we need a whole new _____!

2. You need to weigh these packages on the _____ in the mailroom.

3. This paper is too long. Could you use the _____ to trim it a few inches?

4. My adding machine is broken. I'll have to use my _____.

5. Something is wrong with this _____. I can't hear my boss's voice on this microcassette.

6. This pencil is awfully dull. Where's the _____?

7. For the Board of Directors' meeting, we need to distribute bound annual reports. Please use the _____ to put them together.

8. This brochure needs to look like it's professionally typeset. We need to print it on a _____.

9. Thirty years ago, we did all our correspondence and reports on a _____. Now we use a _____.

10. Ms. Davis wants this report to look like it's typed on a good quality typewriter. Print it on a _____.

11. John Singer in our West Coast office needs to review and sign this contract as soon as possible. Send him a copy on the _____.

12. Sitting in front of a _____ all day can give a person eye strain.

13. Before you put these top secret reports in the recycling bin, be sure to put them through the _____.

B. WHICH CAME FIRST?

Circle the piece of office equipment that came first historically.

1. pencil sharpeners *or* electric pencil sharpeners?
2. calculators *or* adding machines?
3. word processors *or* typewriters?
4. fax machines *or* telex machines?
5. dot-matrix printers *or* laser printers?

C. OFFICE ASSOCIATIONS

Decide which office equipment is associated with the items and actions below. There may be more than one possible answer.

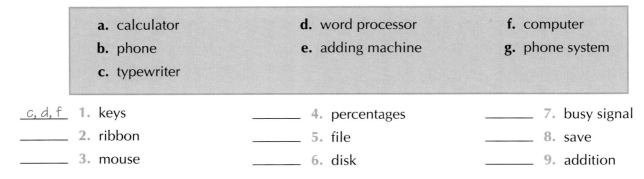

a.	calculator	**d.**	word processor	**f.**	computer
b.	phone	**e.**	adding machine	**g.**	phone system
c.	typewriter				

<u>c, d, f</u> **1.** keys

_____ **2.** ribbon

_____ **3.** mouse

_____ **4.** percentages

_____ **5.** file

_____ **6.** disk

_____ **7.** busy signal

_____ **8.** save

_____ **9.** addition

D. LISTENING: *WHAT ARE THEY TALKING ABOUT?*

Listen and decide what office item is being talked about.

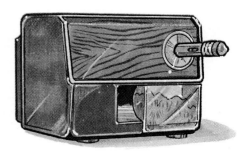

1. **a.** dot-matrix printer
    b. laser printer

2. **a.** fax machine
    b. telephone

3. **a.** pencil sharpener
    b. electric pencil sharpener

4. **a.** postal scale
    b. typewriter

5. **a.** dictaphone
    b. calculator

6. **a.** paper shredder
    b. paper cutter

E. THE LATEST OFFICE INVENTION!

Invent a new piece of office equipment. Give it a name, describe its use, and draw a picture of it in the space below.

A. JANET'S NEW OFFICE

Janet has decided to start her own business. Using the vocabulary on page 88 of the Picture Dictionary, help Janet furnish her new office. She needs:

1. a place to sit, write, and make and receive phone calls   _desk_
2. something to open envelopes
3. something to put pens and pencils in
4. some place to put people's names, addresses, and phone numbers
5. a place to put incoming and outgoing mail
6. something to hold paper clips
7. something to help her remember scheduled meetings
8. something to hold Scotch tape
9. something to keep memos and reminders in
10. something to help her plan her time
11. something to make important parts of reports and memos stand out
12. something to cut things with
13. something to tell her what the date is
14. something on her desk that tells people who she is
15. a place to throw away papers she doesn't want

B. A GOOD IDEA!/NOT A GOOD IDEA!

Decide whether or not the following bits of *office advice* are appropriate.

	A Good Idea	Not a Good Idea
1. You should lean on a desk pad when you write.	✔	___
2. Keep your important files in your tape dispenser.	___	___
3. Use a letter tray to open your letters.	___	___
4. Write all your appointments in your personal planner.	___	___
5. Keep people's names and addresses on your rolodex.	___	___
6. Be sure to use a highlighter pen to sign your letters.	___	___

C. LISTENING: *WHAT ARE THEY TALKING ABOUT?*

Listen and decide what's being talked about.

1. a. desk
   b. swivel chair *(circled)*
2. a. paychecks
   b. desk lamp
3. a. rubber stamp
   b. mechanical pencil
4. a. appointment book
   b. memo holder
5. a. stapler
   b. clipboard
6. a. timesheet
   b. rolodex
7. a. letter opener
   b. punch
8. a. business card
   b. appointment book
9. a. stamp pad
   b. eraser

A. WHAT AM I?

Try to figure out which office supply on page 89 of the Picture Dictionary is *talking*.

1. "Without me, the letters you type are invisible." <u>typing paper</u>

2. "With my help, you get two." _____

3. "I'm white, and I make typographical errors disappear." _____

4. "I'm either blank or have a return address printed on me. You send me on an envelope." _____

5. "I'm often yellow, and I stick without glue or tape." _____

6. "I'm very useful because I stretch around things to hold them together." _____

7. "You need me to print what's on the screen." _____

8. "Because of my name, you might expect to find me only in a law firm, but you can find me everywhere." _____

9. "I'm clear and sticky. From my name, you might think I'm from the United Kingdom." _____

B. WHAT'S THE WORD?

gluestick	mailer	package mailing tape	thumbtack
index card	mailing label	stationery	typewriter ribbon

1. You need to type that letter on official company _____<u>stationery</u>_____.

2. No wonder the words are so light! You need a new _____.

3. A _____ is a special padded envelope you can buy at the post office.

4. I wrote down his address on a 3 x 5 (three inch by five inch) _____.

5. Don't forget to put a _____ on this package.

6. You should probably use _____ to make sure the mailer will be secure.

7. Use a _____ to attach the photographs to the paper.

8. You can fasten that notice to the bulletin board with a _____.

A. ASSOCIATIONS

a. time clock	**d.** lever	**f.** union notice	**i.** assembly line
b. first-aid kit	**e.** warehouse	**g.** cafeteria	**j.** freight elevator
c. safety glasses		**h.** supply room	

_g_ 1. eat   ____ 6. hurt

____ 2. punch in   ____ 7. read

____ 3. store   ____ 8. put on

____ 4. put together   ____ 9. stock

____ 5. pull   ____ 10. load

B. WHAT'S THE WORD?

fire extinguisher	lever	quality control supervisor	suggestion box
first-aid kit	loading dock	safety glasses	supply room
freight elevator	payroll office		

1. To start this machine, pull the ____lever____.

2. You can pick up your checks in the _____.

3. If you run out of glue, look in the _____.

4. The delivery truck is waiting at the _____.

5. To protect their eyes, workers in our factory are required to wear _____.

6. If you have an idea for improving the way we do things, write it down and put it in the _____.

7. I see flames! Where's the _____?

8. In the Shipping Department, we have a very large _____.

9. The fact that our products are so well-made is due in large part to our excellent _____.

10. Quick! There's an emergency! Get the _____!

A. WHAT'S THE OBJECT?

_d_ 1. pneumatic
___ 2. tape
___ 3. frontend
___ 4. dump
___ 5. cement
___ 6. cherry

a. measure
b. mixer
c. picker
d. drill
e. truck
f. loader

B. WHAT'S THE WORD?

blueprints	dump truck	jackhammer	pipe	shingle
brick	hard hat	ladder	plywood	tape measure
bulldozer	insulation	lumber	scaffolding	toolbelt

1. Our architect drew an excellent set of _____blueprints_____ for our new house.

2. Come on! Climb up the _____ to the second floor!

3. Our house has excellent _____. That's why it always stays warm all winter.

4. They dug up the dirt for the foundation with an enormous _____ and removed the dirt in a _____.

5. One of our water _____s burst in the basement and we had a flood!

6. Our carpenter always wears a _____ around her waist.

7. I'm looking for my _____. I need to check the dimensions of the front door.

8. Put on your _____! It's dangerous to work here without one!

9. A sheet of _____ is not very expensive. Good quality _____ costs a lot more.

10. We'll use a _____ to drill that rock.

11. I'm standing outside the top floor of the building on the _____.

12. We have a lovely _____ home.

13. The _____s on our roof have to be replaced.

A. LISTENING: *CALLING ABOUT A CAR*

Listen to the following telephone conversation and circle the answers as you listen.

1. **(a.)** The car costs $700
   b. The car costs $1700.

2. a. The car is a sedan.
   b. The car is a hatchback.

3. a. The fan belt is new.
   b. The car needs a new fan belt.

4. a. The car may need a new clutch.
   b. The car may need new spark plugs.

5. a. The battery stays cold.
   b. The battery is old.

6. a. The air filter can hurt you.
   b. The car probably needs a new air filter.

7. a. The alternator needs to be checked.
   b. The carburetor needs to be checked.

8. a. The brakes make noise.
   b. The brakes are weak.

9. a. The gas gauge is in *tip top* shape, but the defroster doesn't work.
   b. Neither the gas gauge nor the defroster work.

10. a. The horn and the warning lights are working.
    b. The horn and the warning lights don't work.

B. WHICH WORD IS CORRECT?

1. I'm not sure how fast we're going. I'll check the (odometer (speedometer)).

2. The service station attendant lifted the (engine   hood) and checked the oil by looking at the (dipstick   alternator).

3. Don't forget to take the key out of the (steering column   ignition) when you leave your car.

4. I don't like a car with manual transmission because I'm not very good at using a (stickshift   gas pedal) and (dashboard   clutch).

5. The weather was wet and foggy, and so I turned on my (windshield wipers   hubcap) and (muffler   rear defroster).

6. I see that the car driving in front of us has a broken (headlight   taillight).

7. I backed into another car and dented my (hood   bumper).

8. The spare tire is in the (trunk   glove compartment).

9. Our car isn't driving very well these days. We're having a problem with the (radiator   seat belt).

10. We need to stop at a service (bay   station) for some gas.

11. To pump the gas, first take the (visor   nozzle) from the (gas   air) pump.

12. The car won't roll down the hill if you use the (accelerator   emergency brake).

C. CROSSWORD PUZZLE

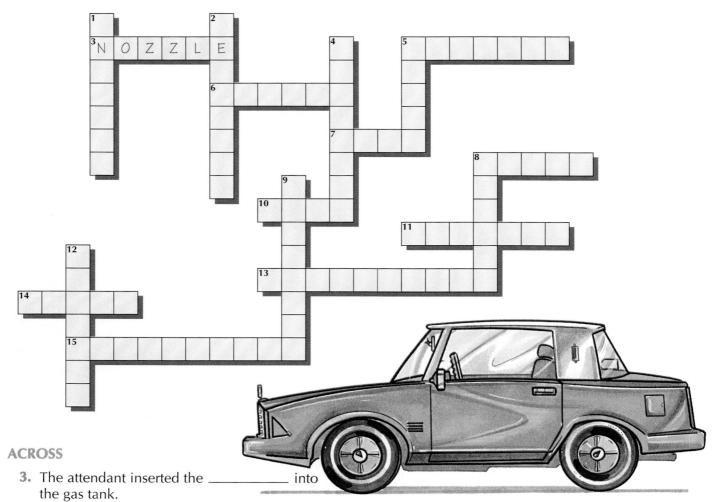

ACROSS

3. The attendant inserted the _____ into the gas tank.

5. The _____ is a continuous rubber belt that drives a fan that keeps the engine cool.

6. The metal covering over the center of the wheel is the _____.

7. You'd better check the air in the rear left _____.

8. Step on the _____! There's something in the middle of the road!

10. Here! Use this _____ to lift up the car.

11. If you want to check the pressure in your tires, the _____ is over there.

13. The _____ mixes gasoline with air so that gas will burn in the cylinders of the engine.

14. It was extremely sunny, and so I lowered the _____ over the windshield.

15. The _____ generates electricity and sends it to the battery.

DOWN

1. The radio reception is very poor. Raise the _____.

2. The _____ fixed all the problems I was having with my car.

4. A _____ is used to measure the amount of oil in the engine.

5. When we had to pull our car over to the side of the road, we immediately lit a _____ to warn other cars.

8. The front and back of every car has _____s to protect the car if it gets hit or *bumped*.

9. The _____ keeps the engine from overheating.

12. Gas is stored in the _____.

A. A GOOD IDEA!/NOT A GOOD IDEA!

Decide whether or not the following driving decisions are appropriate.

	A Good Idea	Not a Good Idea
1. Bob didn't have the correct amount of money, so he got into the exact change lane at the tollbooth.	___	✔
2. Howard likes to drive on the shoulder of the highway.	___	___
3. Margaret slowed down when she saw the yield sign.	___	___
4. I'll stop at the service area to get gas.	___	___
5. Alan drove through the divider to get from one side of the highway to the other.	___	___
6. Since I drive a little slowly, I always drive in the left lane.	___	___
7. Barbara didn't pass the car in front of her because there was a solid line dividing the road.	___	___
8. We're approaching an intersection. Why don't you speed up?	___	___
9. Turn left when you see this sign:	___	___
10. Take that entrance ramp to get onto the interstate.	___	___
11. Do you see that "do not enter" sign? Let's go down that street and see what's there!	___	___
12. Slow down! We're approaching a school crossing.	___	___
13. Let's stop our car on the bridge and admire the view!	___	___
14. Look at the route sign to see what road we're on.	___	___
15. Get into the left lane if you want to pass that car.	___	___
16. Honk your horn while you're driving through the tunnel.	___	___
17. Look both ways at the railroad crossing!	___	___
18. Let's stop our car on the median and rest for awhile!	___	___

B. LISTENING TO DIRECTIONS

Listen and fill in the missing directional information.

1. Take the _____interstate_____ north.

2. You'll see signs for Flagstaff after a _____.

3. Get in the _____ lane and take Exit _____, Maple Street.

4. Immediately after the intersection, there's a _____.

5. Take a right after the railroad crossing onto a _____.

6. After you go over a small _____, the school is at the first _____.

DIRECTIONS TO MY HOUSE

Dear Cousin Juan,

I'm really looking forward to your visit. Unfortunately, it's a bit complicated to get to my house from the airport, so be sure to bring these directions.

When you get your (luggage compartment (baggage))[1], go out front and wait at the (bus   bus stop)[2] for the shuttle (bus stop   bus)[3] that departs every few minutes for the (subway station   commuter)[4]. Buy a (fare box   token)[5] at the (token booth   turnstile)[6] and go through the (token booth   turnstile)[7], following signs that read INBOUND. Take the subway to the (train station   fare)[8], where you'll buy a ticket at the (arrival and departure board   ticket window)[9]. The ticket seller can give you information about the (passenger   schedule)[10]. Consult the (track   arrival and departure board)[11] to see which (timetable   track)[12] the train to Concord leaves from. Depending on how much luggage you bring, you may need help carrying it. (Passengers   Porters)[13] are available to help people with their luggage. After you board the train, the (engineer   conductor)[14] will collect your ticket. When you get to Concord, you'll need to call a (taxicab   taxi stand)[15] using the pay phone in front of the station. The (fare   fare card)[16] is about $5, but be sure to watch the (meter   transfer)[17]. Give the (rider   car driver)[18] my address, and I'll see you whenever you get here. Good luck!

Love,
Carmen

A. A FRUSTRATING FLIGHT!

Complete the following using words from page 96 of the Picture Dictionary.

What a flight! From beginning to end it was a disaster! When I arrived at the airport, there was a huge line at the _____ticket counter_____ [1]. There was only one _____ [2], and it was apparently his first day on the job. The _____ [3] wasn't working, so nobody knew whether flights would be leaving on time or not. Finally, I checked my luggage and went to the _____ [4]. My hand luggage went through the _____ [5] without any problem. Unfortunately, the _____ [6] buzzed when I walked through. After the _____ [7] had me remove my watch and jewelry, I was able to pass through. At the _____ [8] counter, I showed the agent my _____ [9], but she claimed that my seat had already been taken and the plane was overbooked. She suggested that I sit in the _____ [10] while she looked into the matter. Meanwhile, all the other passengers were told to proceed to the _____ [11] to board the plane. After everyone had boarded, they managed to find me a seat in the rear of the plane, right next to the rest rooms. After a very turbulent flight, we finally reached our destination. I went to _____ [12], where a customs official told me that I had not filled out the _____ [13] properly and would have to redo it before she could stamp my _____ [14]. After this was taken care of, I went to the _____ [15] to find my luggage. I had had two suitcases and a garment bag. However, one of my suitcases was missing. I showed my _____ [16] to a ticket agent, but there was nothing he could do. Twenty-four hours later, I had to go back to the airport to pick up my suitcase. It was found, but it also had a big rip in it. I'll never fly that airline again!

B. ANALOGIES

1. porter : skycap *as* snack bar : _____concession stand_____

2. security checkpoint : security guard *as* ticket counter : _____.

3. arrival and departure monitor : Check-In *as* waiting area : _____

4. customs : passport *as* gate : _____

5. tickets : ticket counter *as* baggage : _____

A. PROBABLE OR IMPROBABLE?

Decide whether the following are probable or improbable. Mark those that are probable with a **P** and those that are improbable with an **I**.

__I__ 1. This is your pilot, Captain Hawkins, speaking from the galley.

____ 2. You can store this carry-on bag in the lavatory.

____ 3. The passenger pushed the call button to get the flight attendant.

____ 4. The plane lowered its landing gear as it approached the airport.

____ 5. In case of emergency, turn on the air sickness bag.

____ 6. We sat in the aisle during the whole flight.

____ 7. The pilot never turned on the Fasten Seat Belt sign because the landing was so smooth.

____ 8. If you want a good view from the airplane, I recommend that you ask for a window seat.

____ 9. Because of the emergency, the pilot instructed the passengers to lower their armrests and put on their emergency instruction cards.

____ 10. You'll find your meal in the seat pocket in front of you.

____ 11. The airplane landed on the runway inside the control tower.

____ 12. We put our tray tables in an upright position during take-off.

____ 13. Life vests are an important safety feature on airplanes.

____ 14. There wasn't any room in the first-class section or the cabin, so the passenger sat on the wing.

B. WHICH WORD DOESN'T BELONG?

1. pilot   (instrument panel)   co-pilot   flight engineer
2. armrest   oxygen mask   No Smoking sign   Fasten Seat Belt sign
3. life vest   emergency exit   cargo door   oxygen mask
4. aisle   window   seat belt   middle
5. nose   tail   fuselage   jet
6. jet   prop   rotor   helicopter
7. passenger   galley   flight attendant   captain

C. WHICH WORD?

1. The ((pilot) passenger) turned on the No Smoking sign.
2. Please fasten your (middle seat   seat belt) before take-off!
3. I think I'll put my briefcase in the overhead (pocket   compartment).
4. Ladies and gentlemen, there's a problem in the rear of the airplane. We think the problem is in the (nose   tail).
5. There are many more seats in the (cabin   galley) than in the first-class section.
6. The co-pilot and flight engineer sit in the (instrument panel   cockpit) along with the pilot.

A. WEATHER TALK

cloudy	foggy	lightning	snowstorm	thunderstorm
drizzling	hurricane	muggy	sunny	

1. It's a clear _____ sunny _____ day. Let's go to the beach!

2. It isn't raining very hard. It's just _____.

3. I don't like it when the sky is gray and _____.

4. My hair gets frizzy when it's _____.

5. I hear it's going to be freezing tomorrow and we're going to have a big _____.

6. My children always hold their ears when there's a loud _____.

7. What a terrible _____! All the trees in our neighborhood were destroyed.

8. Look up at the sky! Did you see that flash of _____?

9. I'll open the blinds to see if it's clear or foggy today. Oh! It's _____. I can't see a thing!

B. A GOOD IDEA! / NOT A GOOD IDEA!

1. A. It's windy. I think I'll fly my kite.
   B. (a.) That's a good idea.
      b. I'm not so sure you should.

2. A. It's sleeting. Why don't we have a picnic?
   B. a. That's a wonderful idea!
      b. Let's wait until another time.

3. A. It's freezing. I'll turn on the heat.
   B. a. Please do.
      b. I wouldn't recommend that.

4. A. It's hazy today. I'll definitely need my rubbers and umbrella.
   B. a. I agree. You will.
      b. I don't think you'll need them.

5. A. It's getting muggy. Let's turn off the air conditioning.
   B. a. I hope you do.
      b. Please don't.

6. A. There's going to be a tornado today. Let's go outdoors and watch it.
   B. a. What a great idea!
      b. I think we should stay indoors.

7. A. It's hailing! Let's go sailing!
   B. a. Are you out of your mind?!
      b. I'd love to.

8. A. Let's look at the stars tonight. It's going to be clear.
   B. a. What a good idea!
      b. We won't be able to see a thing!

9. A. Get the suntan lotion! It's drizzling!
   B. a. Good idea!
      b. Suntan lotion?! We need an umbrella!

10. A. They're predicting a thunderstorm tomorrow. We should cancel our barbecue.
    B. a. Why?
       b. I guess we should.

11. A. It's 30 degrees Fahrenheit. Let's go to the beach!
    B. a. What a nice idea!
       b. Don't you think it's a little cold to go to the beach?

A. ASSOCIATIONS

_c_ 1. pitch   a. hatchet

____ 2. carry   b. lantern

____ 3. cook   c. tent

____ 4. chop   d. thermos

____ 5. tie   e. hiking boots

____ 6. climb   f. trail map

____ 7. drink   g. backpack

____ 8. light   h. rope

____ 9. follow   i. camp stove

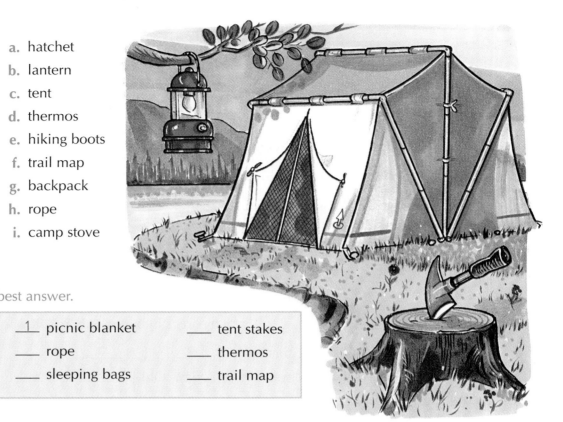

B. LISTENING

Listen and choose the best answer.

____ backpacks	_1_ picnic blanket	____ tent stakes
____ camp stove	____ rope	____ thermos
____ compass	____ sleeping bags	____ trail map

C. THE RIGHT RESPONSE

_f_ 1. Where's the soda?

____ 2. How will we see at night?

____ 3. What will we do to hold up our tent?

____ 4. I don't have any special shoes for hiking.

____ 5. What do you do with your camping gear?

____ 6. Where will we keep the food?

____ 7. Sometimes I get lost in the woods.

____ 8. Don't forget the rope and harness!

____ 9. Do we need to take a camp stove on our camping trip?

a. I won't. They're very important for mountain climbing.

b. We'll bring along a lantern.

c. Tent stakes, of course!

d. I put it all in my backpack.

e. I don't. I always take a compass and trail map with me.

f. In the thermos.

g. In the picnic basket.

h. You really need to get hiking boots.

i. Of course we do! How else can we cook our food?

A. WHAT'S THE WORD?

band shell	merry-go-round	rest room	trash can
bike rack	monkey bars	sand	wading pool
bridle path	picnic area	sandbox	water fountain
jogging path	playground	statue	zoo

1. Let's eat in the _____ *picnic area* _____.

2. There's going to be a concert tonight at the _____.

3. I think I'll run on the _____ while my wife rides her horse on the
   _____.

4. Throw that paper away in the _____!

5. Don't worry. Your children will be safe. The _____ is very shallow.

6. Look! There's the _____ of George Washington!

7. I love to go around and around on the _____ and listen to the organ music.

8. I have to go to the bathroom. Is there a _____ nearby?

9. You can get a drink from that _____ over there.

10. You ought to leave your bicycle at the _____ while we're in the park.

11. I love to look at all the monkeys in the _____.

12. My daughter wants to climb on the _____. How late is the
    _____ open?

13. Jimmy! Don't throw the _____ out of the _____!

B. LISTENING: *WHERE ARE THEY?*

Listen and decide where these people are.

___ on the jogging path	___ in the picnic area	___ on the merry-go-round
___ in the playground	___ on the bridle path	_1_ near the band shell

A. CAN YOU FIND . . .?

Look through the list of words on page 101 of the Picture Dictionary and see if you can find . . .

4 things to sit or lie on.

_____lifeguard stand_____

_____

_____

_____

5 people at the beach.

_____

_____

_____

_____

_____

4 things to protect you from the sun.

_____

_____

_____

_____

4 beach toys.

_____

_____

_____

_____

4 things we use in the water.

_____

_____

_____

_____

4 things we wear or put on.

_____

_____

_____

_____

B. WHICH WORD IS CORRECT?

1. Brr! The water was freezing! Where's my ((towel) blanket) so I can dry off?

2. Oh, no! I don't want to get my hair wet, and I forgot my (sun hat   bathing cap)!

3. If we put up the (beach chair   beach umbrella), we can have some shade.

4. Let's collect some (sand dunes   seashells) when we go to Florida.

5. Tommy, aren't you thirsty? I put some juice in the (cooler   vendor).

6. Please don't talk to the (life preserver   lifeguard). She needs to pay attention to the (swimmers   sunbathers) in the water.

7. George is really going fast on that (air mattress   surfboard)! I hope he doesn't get hurt!

8. Let's get something to eat at the (snack bar   sand castle).

9. The lifeguard is sitting on the (lifeguard seat   lifeguard stand).

10. Do you want to take a walk on the (sand dunes   waves) over there?

11. I love to use a (shovel   kickboard) in the water.

12. Look at that (rock   kite) up in the sky!

13. Put on your (sunglasses   bathing suit). The sun is very bright today.

14. There are very strong (surfers   waves) in the ocean today. I think a storm is coming.

15. My friends and I love to throw a beach (ball   umbrella) back and forth on the beach.

16. Come on, let's go to the beach today! Get your (swimmer   swimsuit)!

C. WHAT'S THE OBJECT?

_e_	1. sand	a.	cap
___	2. lifeguard	b.	towel
___	3. life	c.	lotion
___	4. beach	d.	mattress
___	5. suntan	e.	dune
___	6. bathing	f.	hat
___	7. sun	g.	stand
___	8. air	h.	preserver

D. WHAT'S THE ACTION?

_f_	1. dig	a.	beach umbrella
___	2. surf	b.	sunscreen
___	3. fly	c.	surfboard
___	4. throw	d.	shells
___	5. build	e.	kite
___	6. put up	f.	shovel
___	7. sell	g.	sand castle
___	8. collect	h.	vendor
___	9. put on	i.	beach ball

E. LIKELY OR UNLIKELY?

	Likely	Unlikely
1. The sand dunes are very high in the water today.	___	✔
2. I stepped on a rock in the water and hurt my foot.	___	___
3. Lucy filled a bucket with water.	___	___
4. My son worked as a sunbather at the beach last summer.	___	___
5. To protect herself from the sun, Maria always uses a cooler.	___	___
6. They spent time looking for seashells at the beach.	___	___
7. My daughter was knocked over by an enormous wave.	___	___
8. I wear a bathing cap when I go swimming so my bathing suit won't get wet.	___	___
9. Uncle Walter enjoys lying on a raft in the water.	___	___
10. I live in a beautiful sand castle at the beach.	___	___
11. A common tongue twister is: "She sells seashells by the seashore."	___	___

INDIVIDUAL SPORTS AND RECREATION

A. "OUT OF PLACE"

Which sports DON'T belong in the following categories?

1. Sports you play with a ball:
   bowling
   (running)
   ping pong
   (skateboarding)

2. Sports you play with a glove:
   boxing
   bowling
   handball
   karate

3. Sports that use a net:
   frisbee
   golf
   ping pong
   tennis

4. Sports with at least two players:
   weightlifting
   tennis
   racquetball
   cycling

5. Sports played only indoors:
   golf
   bowling
   skateboarding
   skydiving

6. Sports played on a table:
   pool
   handball
   ping pong
   darts

7. Sports played only outdoors:
   roller skating
   running
   frisbee
   racquetball

B. ANALOGIES

1. racquet : squash as _____paddle_____ : ping pong
2. club : golf as _____ : billiards
3. jogging suit : jogging as _____ : boxing
4. safety goggles : racquetball as _____ : cycling
5. knee pads : roller skating as _____ : skateboarding

C. WHAT AM I?

1.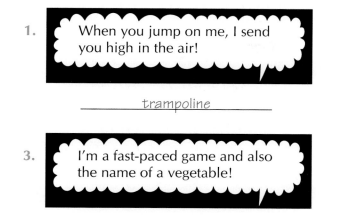
   When you jump on me, I send you high in the air!

   trampoline

2. I bring you safely back to earth!

   _____

3. I'm a fast-paced game and also the name of a vegetable!

   _____

4. Ouch! I just got hit _dead center_ by a bow and arrow!

   _____

D. NAME THAT SPORT!

How many of the following sports facts do you know?

1. Name a sport played in an _alley_.

   bowling

2. Name a sport that requires a pilot.

   _____

3. Name 2 sports that require holes.

   _____
   _____

4. Name 3 sports that require wheels.

   _____
   _____
   _____

5. Name a sport in which you get pinned down on the floor.

   _____

6. Name a sport in which you can get bruised or knocked out.

   _____

7. Name 3 sports that use the floor and walls.

   _____
   _____

8. Name a sport that originated in Asia.

   _____

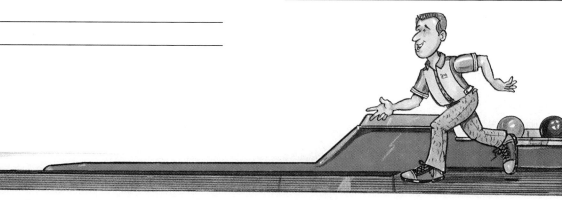

9. Name a sport that was first played on green grass in Scotland.

   _____

10. Name a piece of sports equipment that goes very fast but stays still.

    _____

A. CORRECT OR INCORRECT?

Write **C** if the following names of places are correct or **I** if they are incorrect.

<u>I</u>   1. volleyball field   ____   5. basketball court

____   2. soccer rink   ____   6. hockey rink

____   3. lacrosse field   ____   7. softball field

____   4. football court   ____   8. baseball rink

B. TRUE OR FALSE?

Write **T** if the statement is true or **F** if it is false.

<u>F</u>   1. Baseball players play on a court.

____   2. A hockey rink can melt.

____   3. A football field sometimes has to be mowed.

____   4. A volleyball court has ice on it.

____   5. Lacrosse is played on a hardwood floor.

C. SEARCH FOR THE ANSWER

```
B A S E B A L L  C O U L R G
R F O O T B A L L T M E A R
O R F B A S K E T B A L L P
H O T G O R A R C O U R T L
O R B A L L F I E L D V O A
C R A G A P G K B C E A R Y
K L L S O C C E R B A L E E
E M L V O L L E Y B A L L R
Y A S B R L A C R O S S E H
P Y L O R I N K P A R M Y L
```

1. _____<u>Baseball</u>_____ is the national American pastime.

2. Baseball and _____ are played on a _____.

3. In the United States, this sport is called _____. In other parts of the world it's called _____.

4. _____ is played on skates. It's played on a _____.

5. _____ attracts very tall athletes. It's played on a _____.

6. _____ is also played on a court.

7. You can't use your hands when you play _____.

A. SENSE OR NONSENSE?

Decide whether or not the following make sense.

	Sense	Nonsense
1. Billy, if you're going to play baseball, you need to bring your stick.	___	✔
2. Tom is the catcher. This mask is for him.	___	___
3. The coach told the hockey team not to forget their helmets.	___	___
4. Our volleyball team won because Mary's serve hit the backboard.	___	___
5. Jim lost several lacrosse pucks this season.	___	___
6. Julie plays on the school softball team. For her birthday, her mother gave her a new mitt.	___	___
7. They had to stop the basketball game because one of the players' shoulder pads fell off.	___	___
8. It's important to have a good hockey hoop.	___	___

B. WHO'S TALKING?

_c_ 1. baseball player

___ 2. football player

___ 3. hockey player

___ 4. lacrosse player

___ 5. basketball player

___ 6. volleyball player

___ 7. soccer player

a. There's the puck. Go after it!

b. Oh, no! The ball touched the net!

c. I've got my mitt and my helmet, and I'm all ready for the game!

d. This helmet and my heavy padded uniform protect me when I play this rough sport.

e. I couldn't play a match without these shinguards.

f. I wear this face guard whenever I play.

g. I think I can actually touch the hoop with my hands!

C. LISTENING

Listen and decide which answer is correct.

1. a. mask
   b. mitt (circled)

2. a. board
   b. guard

3. a. ball
   b. net

4. a. helmet
   b. stick

5. a. soccer team
   b. hockey team

6. a. baseball
   b. soccer ball

7. a. gloves
   b. helmets

8. a. baseball uniforms
   b. baseball guards

WINTER SPORTS AND RECREATION

A. WHAT'S THE OBJECT?

_d_	1. ski	a.	skates
___	2. bob	b.	sled
___	3. snow	c.	skis
___	4. sledding	d.	boots
___	5. cross-country	e.	guards
___	6. ice	f.	dish
___	7. skate	g.	mobile

B. WHAT'S THE SPORT?

Which sports on page 106 of the Picture Dictionary would need the following? (There may be more than one possible answer for each.)

1. poles   _downhill skiing, cross-country skiing_
2. a frozen pond   _____
3. a hill   _____
4. ankle support   _____
5. sharp blades   _____
6. a chair lift   _____
7. mountainous terrain   _____
8. gasoline   _____

C. WHAT'S YOUR OPINION?

Tell about the sports on page 106 of the Picture Dictionary.

1. In your opinion, which is the most difficult? Why?

. . . .

2. Which is the easiest? Why?

. . . .

3. Which is the most dangerous? Why?

. . . .

4. Which is the safest? Why?

. . . .

5. Which is the most beautiful to watch? Why?

. . . .

6. Which do you think is the most expensive? Why?

. . . .

A. ASSOCIATIONS

_f_	1. hair	a. canoe
___	2. breathe	b. bathing suit
___	3. swim	c. fishing rod
___	4. feet	d. life preserver
___	5. pull	e. air tank
___	6. paddle	f. bathing cap
___	7. protect	g. flippers
___	8. see	h. towrope
___	9. bait	i. goggles

B. WHAT DO YOU WEAR?

_c_	1. You wear a snorkel	a. over your eyes.
___	2. You wear flippers	b. on your head.
___	3. You wear a mask	c. in your mouth.
___	4. You wear goggles	d. on your back.
___	5. You wear a bathing cap	e. on your feet.
___	6. You wear an air tank	f. over your face.

C. WHAT'S THE SPORT?

a. canoeing   c. rowing   e. snorkeling   g. water skiing
b. fishing   d. scuba diving   f. swimming   h. windsurfing

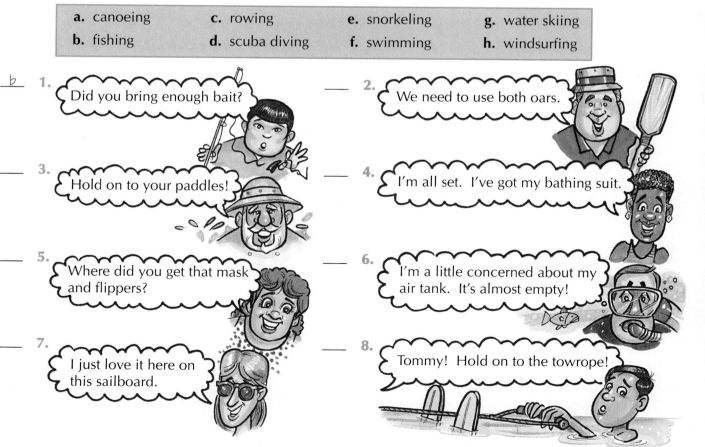

_b_ 1. Did you bring enough bait?

2. We need to use both oars.

3. Hold on to your paddles!

4. I'm all set. I've got my bathing suit.

5. Where did you get that mask and flippers?

6. I'm a little concerned about my air tank. It's almost empty!

7. I just love it here on this sailboard.

8. Tommy! Hold on to the towrope!

A. WHAT DO YOU DO?

_c_ 1. You hit, pitch, and catch when you _____.

____ 2. You throw, pass, and kick when you _____.

____ 3. You serve when you _____.

____ 4. You dribble, shoot, and bounce the ball when you _____.

____ 5. You do jumping jacks, leg-lifts, and deep-knee bends when you _____.

____ 6. You do somersaults, cartwheels, and handstands when you _____.

a. do aerobics
b. do gymnastics
c. play baseball
d. play basketball
e. play football
f. play tennis

B. WHAT'S THE ACTION?

bend	bounce	dive	kick	reach	serve	stretch
catch	hop	pitch	run	shoot	swim	

1. Collins really knows how to _____shoot_____ a basketball. He gets it into the hoop every time.

2. In soccer, you aren't allowed to touch the ball, only _____ it.

3. Billy, please don't _____ the ball up and down! It makes too much noise and your sister can't sleep.

4. I'm teaching my son how to _____ the ball with his glove when I _____ it to him.

5. In my opinion, any tennis player can hit the ball over the net, but very few really know how to _____ it well.

6. To enter a marathon, you really have to like to _____.

7. Can you _____ up and down on one foot?

8. I have trouble _____ing since my knee operation.

9. Lift your arms and _____ up high.

10. I love to _____ in the pool down the street. However, I don't like to _____ because it's too dangerous.

11. Come on! _____ those muscles!

WHAT'S THE WORD?

astronomy	coin collecting	Monopoly	pottery	stamp collecting
bird watching	crocheting	painting	sculpting	weaving
cards	knitting	photography	sewing	woodworking
chess	model building			

1. My hobby is _____painting_____. Here are my brushes and easel.

2. I'm feeling frustrated. I've got my needles and thread, but my _____ machine is broken.

3. This wool sweater you made is beautiful. How long have you been _____?

4. I love _____. On weekends I can sit at my loom for hours.

5. I'd like to spend this morning _____, but I can't find my hook.

6. I really like this bookcase that Jack built. He has incredible _____ skills.

7. My husband's hobby is making _____. He has a gigantic wheel in the other room. He's made some beautiful painted clay dishes.

8. I feel like _____ today. Where did you put the plaster and clay?

9. My son has been interested in _____ for many years. He has a complete collection of twentieth century silver dollars.

10. I just bought a new pair of binoculars. Let's go _____ this Sunday.

11. _____ is a famous board game in which people use special *play* money to buy and sell property.

12. Many young people enjoy _____. With a kit, some glue, and some paint, they can create authentic miniature cars and planes.

13. If you're interested in knowing more about _____, talk with the manager of the post office.

14. My daughter's hobby is _____. She's saving money to buy a telescope.

15. With that magnificent camera, I'm sure you can do some wonderful _____.

16. I enjoy playing _____. My favorite game is bridge.

17. _____ and checkers are similar games. They're both played on a square checkered board.

A. WHAT'S HAPPENING THIS WEEKEND?

actor	balcony	box office	lobby	theater
actress	ballet dancer	conductor	scenery	ticket
audience	ballet company	lighting	stage	

ENTERTAINMENT UPDATE

"A lot is happening on _____ stage _____[1] this weekend. First, for _____[2] lovers, last season's most successful Broadway hit is now playing to enthusiastic _____[3]s here. From start to finish, this show is a smash! The _____[4] and _____[5] effects are impressive, and the _____[6]s and _____[7]es put on fine performances. _____[8]s are still available for _____[9] seats for tonight's show by calling the theater _____[10]. Also this weekend, *Swan Lake* will be performed, featuring an exciting new _____[11] headed by the world-famous _____[12] Misha Barikov. Music lovers will enjoy the season's final symphony performance. Wielding his baton for the last time this year will be the renowned _____[13] Kenji Hirasawa. Be sure to stop to see the fine art of local artists in the Symphony Hall _____[14] and refreshment area while you are there. That's the entertainment update for this weekend."

B. LISTENING

Listen and choose the best answer.

1. a. spotlight
   b. stage

2. a. audience
   b. program

3. a. marquee
   b. screen

4. a. chorus
   b. ballet company

5. a. orchestra pit
   b. orchestra

6. a. baton
   b. podium

7. a. refreshment stand
   b. box office

8. a. actor
   b. usher

A. WHAT'S ON TV?

Match the types of TV programs with their descriptions. Then fill in the name of a television program you know for each type.

sitcom	news program	drama	children's program	sports program
game show	music video	variety show	talk show	cartoon

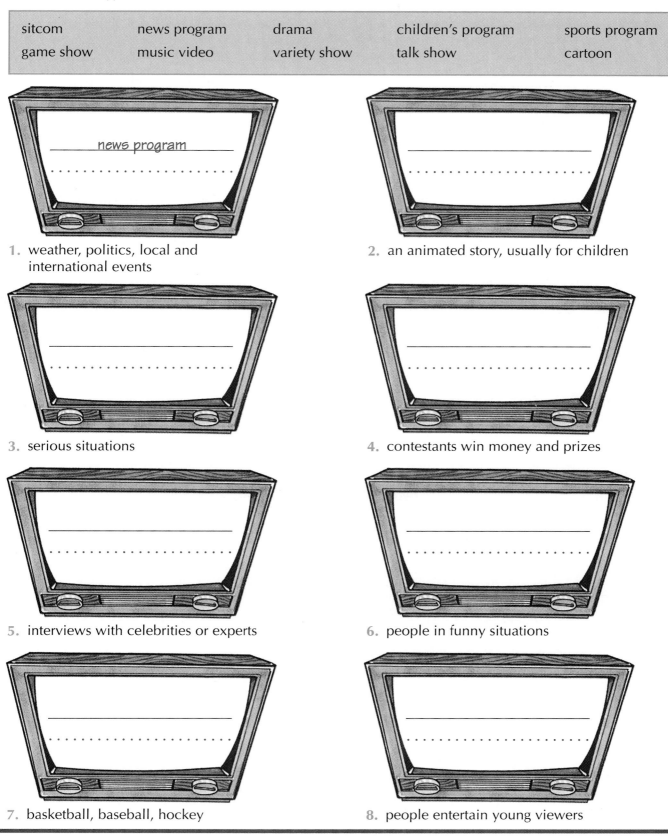

1. weather, politics, local and international events

news program

2. an animated story, usually for children

3. serious situations

4. contestants win money and prizes

5. interviews with celebrities or experts

6. people in funny situations

7. basketball, baseball, hockey

8. people entertain young viewers

B. WHAT'S AT THE MOVIES?

drama	cartoon	western	adventure movie
comedy	war movie	foreign film	science fiction movie

1. A classic _____western_____ about a cowboy who falls in love.

2. The special effects in this futuristic _____ are remarkable!

3. This Czech movie is the most popular _____ of the year. See it today!

4. *The Magic Bubble* is the best Disney film in years. It's more than just a _____!

5. The Viet Nam conflict has never been so realistically depicted. A magnificent _____!

6. A beautiful and talented violinist contracts a fatal virus. What a tearful _____!

7. A classic Marx Brothers _____! You won't stop laughing!

8. A suspenseful and exciting _____! Oklahoma Holmes faces danger every action-filled minute!

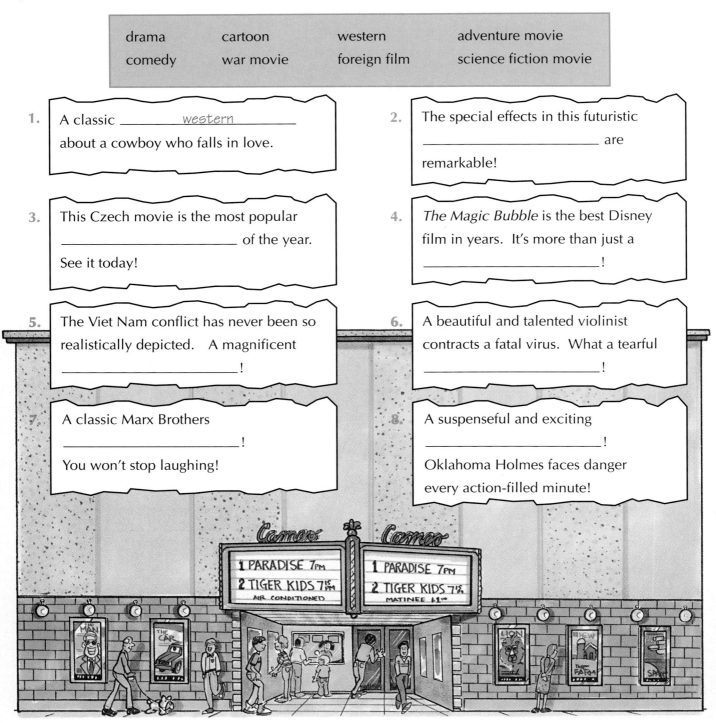

C. LISTENING

Listen and put a number next to the type of music you hear.

____ gospel music	__1__ classical music	____ reggae
____ rock music	____ country music	____ rap music
____ folk music	____ blues	____ jazz

A. WHICH INSTRUMENT DOESN'T BELONG?

1. electric guitar   (drum)   bass   harp
2. bongos   cymbals   drum   accordion
3. banjo   trumpet   tuba   trombone
4. piccolo   cello   oboe   flute
5. piano   synthesizer   organ   bassoon

B. LIKELY OR UNLIKELY?

		Likely	Unlikely
1.	My son wanted to take a percussion instrument, so I decided to give him piano lessons.	___	✔
2.	That band has a beautiful harp.	___	___
3.	Our orchestra has string instruments.	___	___
4.	Those cymbals are very quiet. They hardly make any noise.	___	___
5.	I just plugged in my electric guitar.	___	___
6.	I couldn't play my harmonica because my foot was broken.	___	___
7.	I love to hear the organ music in church.	___	___
8.	That string quartet had a viola, a bass, a tuba, and a cello.	___	___

C. ASSOCIATIONS

_f_ 1. violin   **a.** Hawaii
___ 2. electric guitar   **b.** woodwind
___ 3. bongos   **c.** church
___ 4. ukelele   **d.** rock band
___ 5. oboe   **e.** mouth
___ 6. harmonica   **f.** strings
___ 7. organ   **g.** drums

D. LISTENING: *WHAT'S THAT SOUND?*

Listen and decide what musical instrument you're listening to.

___ piano   ___ harmonica   ___ trumpet
___ drums   ___ cymbals   ___ organ
___ flute   _1_ violin   ___ guitar

TREES, FLOWERS, AND PLANTS

A. CATEGORIES

Write the words under the correct categories.

bark	daffodil	maple	stamen
birch	daisy	oak	stem
bud	leaf	petal	trunk
cherry	limb	petunia	tulip

Parts of a flower:

_____petal_____

_____

_____

_____

Parts of a tree:

_____

_____

_____

_____

Types of flowers:

_____

_____

_____

_____

Types of trees:

_____

_____

_____

_____

B. WHAT AM I?

Decide which of the trees, flowers, or plants on page 113 of the Picture Dictionary is *talking*.

> I'm reddish-green, and I can make people break out in a rash.

1. _____poison ivy_____

> Send a dozen red ones on Valentine's Day to show someone you love them.

2. _____

> I'm a big tree that looks like it's crying.

3. _____

> I'm the flower or leaf before it opens.

4. _____

> I'm a very common green weed that is often mowed.

5. _____

> Coconuts grow on me, and I'm only found in warm climates.

6. _____

> If you pick a rose, you may prick yourself on me.

7. _____

> I'm a very large coniferous tree that grows in California.

8. _____

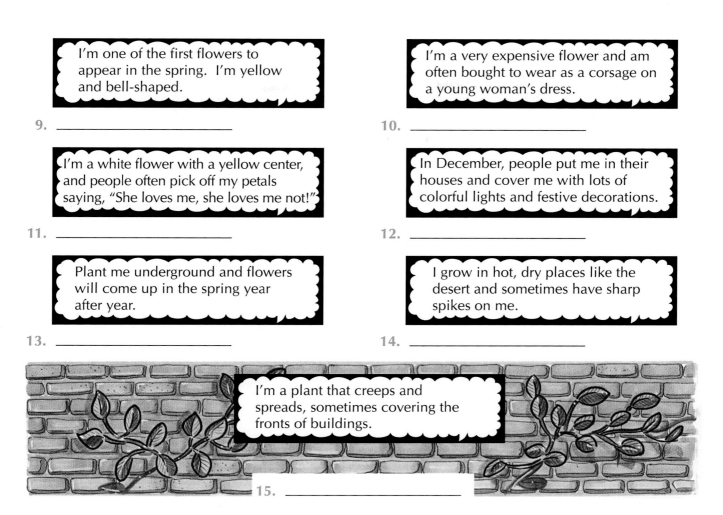

I'm one of the first flowers to appear in the spring. I'm yellow and bell-shaped.

9. _____

I'm a very expensive flower and am often bought to wear as a corsage on a young woman's dress.

10. _____

I'm a white flower with a yellow center, and people often pick off my petals saying, "She loves me, she loves me not!"

11. _____

In December, people put me in their houses and cover me with lots of colorful lights and festive decorations.

12. _____

Plant me underground and flowers will come up in the spring year after year.

13. _____

I grow in hot, dry places like the desert and sometimes have sharp spikes on me.

14. _____

I'm a plant that creeps and spreads, sometimes covering the fronts of buildings.

15. _____

C. DREAM GARDEN

Using the plot plan below, design and label a landscape plan for your *dream garden*.

A. MATCH

_f_ 1. Grand
___ 2. Hoover
___ 3. Death
___ 4. Mojave
___ 5. Great
___ 6. Mississippi
___ 7. Appalachian
___ 8. Redwood
___ 9. Hawaiian
___ 10. Pacific
___ 11. Niagara
___ 12. Walden

a. Falls
b. Islands
c. Ocean
d. Mountains
e. Desert
f. Canyon
g. Lake
h. Forest
i. Pond
j. River
k. Valley
l. Dam

B. WHICH WORD IS CORRECT?

1. In the fairy tale *Hansel and Gretel*, the children get lost in the ((forest) ocean).

2. My sister loves adventure. Recently she rode the (dam   rapids) of the Colorado River in her canoe.

3. It's hard to believe that this little (dune   stream) was once a rushing river.

4. Some people like swimming in pools or fresh-water lakes, but I prefer the (seashore   plateau).

5. Even though I'm afraid of heights, I love hang-gliding off of (rivers   cliffs).

6. When I was a child, I dreamed about tracking panthers and other wild animals in the (jungle   hill).

7. We heat our home with (hydroelectric power   natural gas).

8. I love to hear the crashing sound of a (waterfall   brook).

9. There's no sign of water in this (acid rain   desert).

10. The thing that concerns me most is air (energy   pollution).

C. LISTENING

Listen and choose the best answer.

1. a. pollution
   b. natural gas

2. a. coal
   b. toxic waste

3. a. oil and gas
   b. wind and radiation

4. a. acid rain
   b. hydroelectric power

5. a. rain
   b. radiation

6. a. air pollution
   b. water pollution

7. a. oil
   b. solar energy

8. a. wind
   b. coal

A. WHERE ARE THEY?

henhouse	sty	field	farmhouse
garden	stable	coop	orchard

1. The farmer is in the _____farmhouse_____.
2. The chicken is in the _____.
3. The horse is in the _____.
4. The scarecrow is in the _____.
5. The pig is in the _____.
6. The fruit tree is in the _____.
7. The hen is in the _____.
8. The crop is in the _____.

B. WHICH WORD IS CORRECT?

1. A ((hired hand) silo) assists the farmer.
2. Our (tractor   irrigation system) brings water to areas that would otherwise be dry.
3. A machine that reaps, threshes, and cleans grain is called a (pitchfork   combine).
4. Birds that might eat the crops are kept away by a (scarecrow   fence).
5. You can move that hay with a (stable   pitchfork).
6. The largest (crop   orchard) on our farm is wheat.
7. Most of the cows are grazing in the (garden   pasture).
8. The farmer and his family live in the (hen house   farmhouse).
9. We have several animals in our (barnyard   garden).
10. One of our cows just gave birth to two (bulls   calves).

C. ANIMAL SOUNDS!

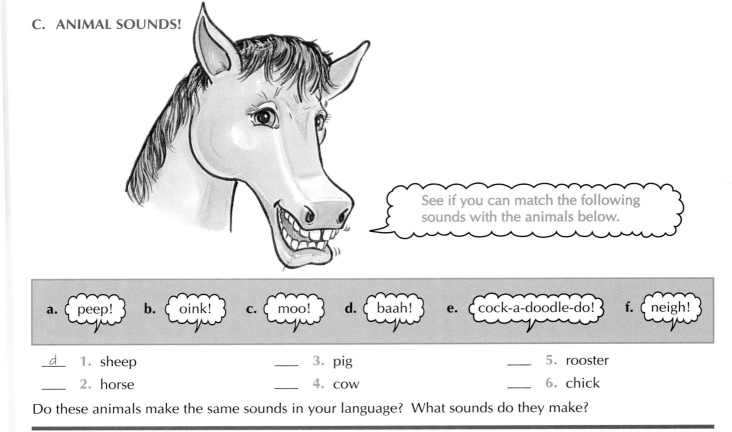

See if you can match the following sounds with the animals below.

a. peep!	b. oink!	c. moo!	d. baah!	e. cock-a-doodle-do!	f. neigh!

_d_	1. sheep	___	3. pig	___	5. rooster
___	2. horse	___	4. cow	___	6. chick

Do these animals make the same sounds in your language? What sounds do they make?

D. CATEGORIES

Decide which farm words on page 115 of the Picture Dictionary belong in the following categories.

Buildings: Areas: Machinery:

_____farmhouse_____   _____   _____

_____   _____   _____

_____   _____

_____   _____

_____   _____

_____   _____

E. ANALOGIES

1. calf : cow *as* kid: _____goat_____

2. combine : crop *as* pitchfork : _____

3. farmer : farmhouse *as* chicken : _____

4. fruit tree : orchard *as* crop : _____

5. pork : pig *as* beef : _____

6. goat : goats *as* sheep : _____

7. turkey : turkeys *as* calf : _____

8. milk : cows *as* eggs : _____

F. WHO'S MY MOTHER?

For the baby animals below, fill in the names of the corresponding adult animals.

1. piglet   _____   4. calf   _____

2. chick   _____   5. foal   _____

3. lamb   _____   6. kid   _____

G. ASSOCIATIONS

_f_ 1. orchard   a. enclose

___ 2. irrigation system   b. protect

___ 3. hired hand   c. assist

___ 4. fence   d. store

___ 5. farmhouse   e. water

___ 6. scarecrow   f. grow

___ 7. silo   g. live

A. ANALOGIES

1. horn : rhinoceros *as* tusk : _____elephant_____
2. stripes : zebra *as* spots : _____
3. pouch : kangaroo *as* hump : _____
4. horse : foal *as* deer : _____
5. mouse : mice *as* wolf : _____
6. cat : whiskers *as* lion : _____

B. WHO'S TALKING?

1. "I have spots and a long, thin neck."   _____giraffe_____
2. "I'm like a horse, but smaller even when I'm full grown."   _____
3. "I'm known as man's best friend."   _____
4. "I have sharp quills all over my body."   _____
5. "I'm called the king of the jungle."   _____
6. "I look like a mouse with wings, and I hang upside down during the day."   _____
7. "I'm black and white and produce a bad odor when I'm threatened."   _____
8. "I'm a large animal known for my big antlers."   _____
9. "I'm a kind of bear with white fur who lives in cold climates."   _____
10. "I'm a boneless creature who can survive even when I'm cut in half."   _____
11. "I carry my newborns in my pouch."   _____
12. "I make a sound that resembles someone laughing."   _____
13. "If you come to Africa and see an animal with a hump – that's me!"   _____
14. "I'm a common household pet whose babies are called *kittens*."   _____
15. "Look for me in the woods. I'll be building a dam."   _____

C. ANIMAL EXPRESSIONS

Certain qualities are attributed to certain animals. See if you can guess which ones they are. Are they the same in your culture?

1. as sly as a _____fox_____
2. as quiet as a _____
3. as stubborn as a _____
4. as strong as a _____
5. as busy as a _____
6. as blind as a _____

Add some of your own.

. . . .

. . . .

A. COLOR ME BEAUTIFUL!

Without looking back at the Picture Dictionary, try to match the colors with the following birds.

<u>f</u> **1.** white   **a.** peacock

____ **2.** pink   **b.** crow

____ **3.** black   **c.** cardinal

____ **4.** black and white   **d.** blue jay

____ **5.** multicolored   **e.** penguin

____ **6.** red   **f.** swan

____ **7.** blue   **g.** flamingo

B. WHO'S TALKING?

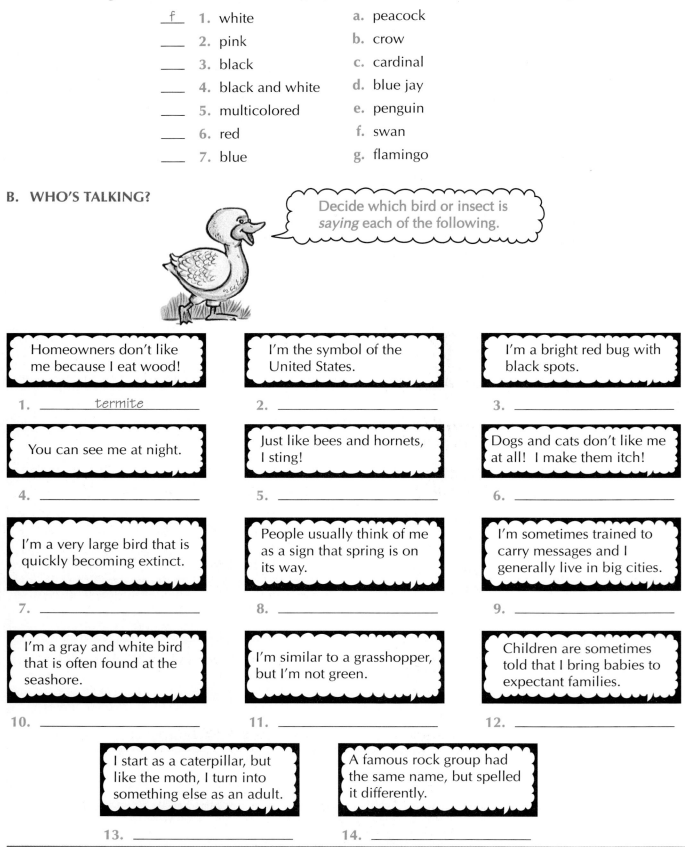

Decide which bird or insect is *saying* each of the following.

Homeowners don't like me because I eat wood!

1. _____termite_____

I'm the symbol of the United States.

2. _____

I'm a bright red bug with black spots.

3. _____

You can see me at night.

4. _____

Just like bees and hornets, I sting!

5. _____

Dogs and cats don't like me at all! I make them itch!

6. _____

I'm a very large bird that is quickly becoming extinct.

7. _____

People usually think of me as a sign that spring is on its way.

8. _____

I'm sometimes trained to carry messages and I generally live in big cities.

9. _____

I'm a gray and white bird that is often found at the seashore.

10. _____

I'm similar to a grasshopper, but I'm not green.

11. _____

Children are sometimes told that I bring babies to expectant families.

12. _____

I start as a caterpillar, but like the moth, I turn into something else as an adult.

13. _____

A famous rock group had the same name, but spelled it differently.

14. _____

A. ASSOCIATIONS

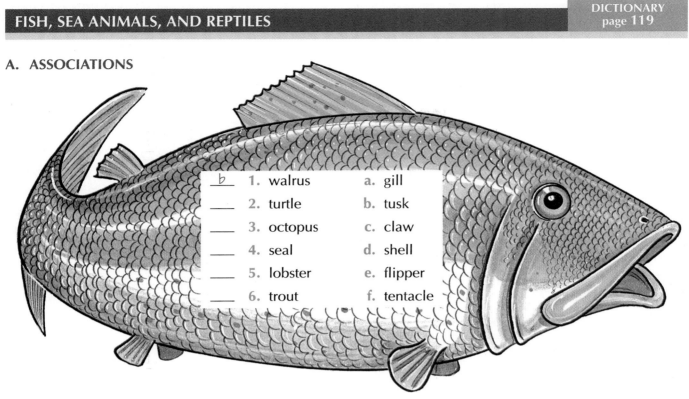

_b_	1. walrus	a.	gill
___	2. turtle	b.	tusk
___	3. octopus	c.	claw
___	4. seal	d.	shell
___	5. lobster	e.	flipper
___	6. trout	f.	tentacle

B. WHICH WORD DOESN'T BELONG?

1. tortoise   (scallop)   turtle   crocodile
2. tentacle   flipper   clam   claw
3. cobra   boa   tadpole   rattlesnake
4. flounder   squid   swordfish   shark
5. dolphin   shrimp   seal   eel
6. gill   shell   fin   tail
7. snail   otter   walrus   whale

C. LISTENING: *AT THE AQUARIUM*

Listen and circle the correct answer.

1. a. There are some amphibians and reptiles on the lower level.
   b. There are some sea animals on the lower level.

2. a. In the tank you can see salmon and tortoises.
   b. In the tank you can see snails and sea horses.

3. a. The least dangerous shark is the *Great White Shark*.
   b. The most dangerous shark is the *Great White Shark*.

4. a. Everybody can tell the difference between crocodiles and alligators.
   b. Many people can't tell the difference between crocodiles and alligators.

5. a. There are both fish and sea animals in the tide pool.
   b. There are fish, but there aren't any sea animals in the tide pool.

6. a. Crabs and lobsters are in the octopus tank.
   b. There are special tanks for lobsters and crabs.

7. a. Dolphins perform for people visiting the aquarium.
   b. Don't go to the whale show. It's only for children.

125

A. 3-D

Complete the following sentences.

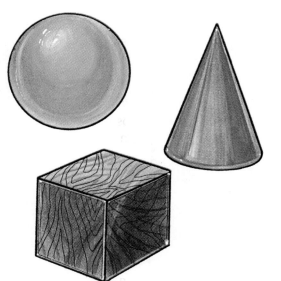

1. Each side of a _____cube_____ is a square.

2. The sides of a _____ are triangles.

3. The two ends of a _____ are circles.

4. The base of a _____ is a circle.

5. A _____ doesn't have a base or a side.

B. WHAT'S THE WORD?

1. There are twelve _____inches_____ in a foot.

2. A mile is equal to 1.6 _____.

3. The _____ between the earth and the sun is 93 million _____.

4. An inch equals 2.54 _____.

5. Three feet is the same as a _____.

6. The orbit followed by the planets is shaped like an _____.

7. The top part of a triangle is its _____.

8. All three sides are of equal length in an _____ triangle.

9. The area of a _____ is its length times its width.

10. The longest side of a right triangle is called its _____.

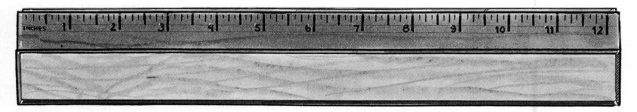

C. WORLDLY SHAPES

Find 5 examples of *real-world* objects for each of the following shapes:

1. cube . . . .

2. cylinder . . . .

3. sphere . . . .

4. cone . . . .

5. pyramid . . . .

A. OUTER SPACE RIDDLES

_n_   **1.** "A million earths could fit inside me. Without me, life on earth would be impossible."

____   **2.** " Humans have walked upon me, but I can't support life. I'm visible most nights."

____   **3.** "I'm the closest planet to the sun and the second smallest in our solar system."

____   **4.** "I'm about the same size as Earth, but I'm too hot to sustain life. I'm named after the Roman goddess of love."

____   **5.** "I'm a constellation of stars shaped like a saucepan, and I have a smaller twin."

____   **6.** "I'm made up of gas, stars, and dust. The one you are most familiar with is called the _Milky Way_."

____   **7.** "I'm the largest planet and I'm known for my colorful stripes."

____   **8.** "I'm a celestial body made up of a solid head and a long vapor tail. People often think of _Halley's_ when they think of me."

____   **9.** "I'm known as a _minor planet_ that orbits around the sun. There are many of me, especially between Mars and Jupiter."

____ **10.** "The second largest planet, I'm surrounded by a series of rings."

____ **11.** "I'm both the smallest planet in our solar system and the farthest from the sun."

____ **12.** "When one celestial body partially or completely obscures another, I occur."

____ **13.** "People used to believe that I, Earth's neighbor, could support life."

____ **14.** "Also known as a _shooting star_, I appear as a luminous trail in the sky."

____ **15.** "The eighth planet from the sun, I have rings and eight satellites."

____ **16.** "I'm the seventh planet from the sun and almost the same size as my neighbor, Neptune."

a. meteor
b. eclipse
c. moon
d. Mercury
e. Big Dipper
f. Venus
g. Mars
h. galaxy
i. Jupiter
j. Pluto
k. Saturn
l. Uranus
m. Neptune
n. sun
o. comet
p. asteroid

B. SPACE EXPLORATION CROSSWORD PUZZLE

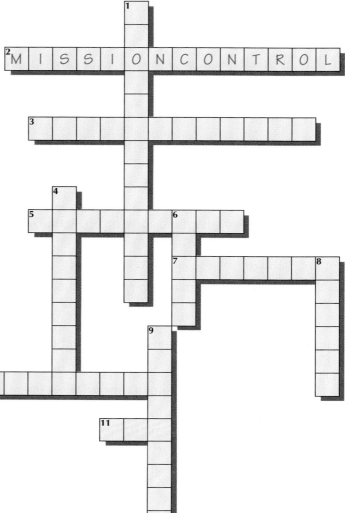

Across 2: MISSIONCONTROL

ACROSS

2. The individuals who control a space flight.

3. A vehicle for carrying people and supplies back and forth from earth to a space station.

5. The base from which a space craft or rocket is sent into space.

7. Another word for space craft.

10. What an astronaut wears in space.

11. The abbreviation for an unidentified flying object.

DOWN

1. A rocket that *boosts* or pushes a space craft into orbit.

4. A man-made object which moves in space for some purpose.

6. An unmanned space craft that explores outer space or other planets and transmits data to earth.

8. An object which travels into space and which is driven by burning gases.

9. A person who is involved with space exploration.

WORKBOOK PAGE 1

A. WHAT'S THE QUESTION?

1. What's your name?
2. What's your first name?
3. What's your middle name?
4. What's your last name?
5. What's your address?
6. What's your zip code?
7. What's your telephone number?
8. What's your social security number?

B. WHAT INFORMATION DO YOU NEED?

1. name, address
2. area code, telephone number
3. name/first name/first name and last name (depending on who you're introducing)
4. address
5. first name, middle name, last name, address, city, state, zip code, area code, telephone number, social security number

C. LISTENING

Listen and choose the correct answer.
A. Tell me your last name again.
B. It's Andrews. My name is Stanley Andrews.
A. And do you have a number where we can reach you, Mr. Andrews?
B. Yes. You can call me at six eight four—one nine nine six.
A. Is that area code two oh nine?
B. Yes. That's right.
A. And where do you live, Mr. Andrews?
B. On fourteen Hudson Road.
A. Is that here in Westerly?
B. No. I live in Easton. And the zip code there is two two four nine oh.
A. Did you say two two nine four oh?
B. No. Two two four nine oh.
A. Well, I think I've got all the information I need. Thank you, Mr. Andrews.
Answers
1. a   4. b
2. b   5. b
3. a   6. a

WORKBOOK PAGE 2

A. WHO ARE THEY?

1. grandfather   6. nephew
2. aunt   7. nieces
3. uncle   8. brother-in-law
4. aunt   9. mother in law
5. cousins   father-in-law

B. RELATIVES

1. c   4. d
2. a   5. b
3. e

C. WHAT'S THE RELATIONSHIP?

1. husband : wife
2. father : daughter
3. sister : brother
4. mother-in-law : daughter-in law
5. aunt : niece
6. grandfather : granddaughter
7. father-in-law : son-in-law
8. grandmother : grandson
9. sister-in-law : sister-in law
10. cousin : cousin

WORKBOOK PAGES 3-4

A. WHERE AM I?

1. Kansas   7. Oregon
2. North Dakota   8. Vermont
3. Costa Rica   9. Sonora
4. British Columbia   10. Louisiana
5. Indiana   11. Cuba
6. North Carolina   12. Pennsylvania

B. NORTH AMERICA GEOGRAPHY QUIZ

1. Alaska
2. They all border the Pacific Ocean.
3. Virginia, Maryland, Delaware, New Jersey, New York, Connecticut, Rhode Island, Massachusetts, New Hampshire
4. Texas, Louisiana, Mississippi, Alabama, Florida
5. Washington, Alaska, Idaho, Montana, North Dakota, Minnesota, Wisconsin, Michigan, New York, Vermont, New Hampshire, Maine
6. British Columbia, Alberta, Saskatchewan, Manitoba, Ontario, Quebec, New Brunswick
7. Minnesota, Wisconsin, Michigan, Illinois, Indiana, Ohio, Pennsylvania, New York

C. WHICH WAY DID THEY GO?

1. east
2. south
3. west
4. north

WORKBOOK PAGES 5–6

A. GEOGRAPHICALLY SPEAKING

1. North America   8. Arctic Ocean
2. Chile   9. Paraguay, Bolivia
3. Madagascar   10. Jamaica, Puerto Rico, Cuba
4. Atlantic Ocean   and Haiti, The Dominican
5. Indian   Republic
6. Sweden   11. Mongolia
7. Austria   12. Sri Lanka

B. GEOGRAPHICAL ASSOCIATIONS

1. China
2. Italy
3. United States
4. Russia
5. Canada
6. Japan
7. Australia
8. India
9. Egypt

C. AROUND THE WORLD

1. f   7. b
2. j   8. g
3. h   9. a
4. m   10. e
5. d   11. c
6. k

D. CAN YOU NAME . . .?

1. Iceland
2. Ukraine, Russia, Georgia, Turkey, Bulgaria, Romania
3. (discuss with others)
4. The United States, Canada, the United Kingdom, Australia, New Zealand, South Africa
5. (see the map of Africa)
6. Russia, Estonia, Latvia, Lithuania, Belarus, Ukraine, Moldova, Georgia, Armenia, Turkmenistan, Uzbekistan, Tajikistan, Kyrgyzstan, Kazakhstan, Azerbaijan

7. Spain, all Central and South American countries except Brazil

WORKBOOK PAGE 7

A. WHICH WORD IS CORRECT?

1. take a bath
2. breakfast
3. taking a shower
4. make
5. teeth
6. make
7. gets up
8. teeth
9. get undressed
10. comb his hair

B. LISTENING

Listen and choose the best answer.

1. Mary went sailing this afternoon. It was very windy and now her hair looks terrible. She really needs to . . . .
2. Joe's alarm clock is ringing. It's seven A.M., and he has to get to work by eight o'clock. "Okay, Joe! It's time to . . . !"
3. My six-year-old niece got chocolate sauce all over her nose and cheeks while she was eating an ice cream sundae. She needs to . . . .
4. George is having an examination at the doctor's office. The doctor is asking him to take off his clothes. "George, it's time to . . . !"
5. Jane is very tired. It's almost midnight, and she has a lot of things to do tomorrow. She really should . . . .
6. It's noon, and Charlie is so busy at the office that he probably won't have time to . . . .
7. Barbara just washed her face and combed her hair. Now it's time to . . . .
8. My thirteen-year-old son is really growing up. Soon he'll be ready to . . . .

Answers

2	1
6	5
4	8
7	3

C. IT'S TIME TO GET UP!

1. up
2. face
3. teeth
4. shower
5. shave
6. hair
7. bed
8. breakfast

WORKBOOK PAGE 8

A. WHAT'S THE ACTIVITY?

1. cleaning
2. dusting
3. vacuuming
4. ironing
5. practices the piano
6. plays basketball
7. studying
8. read
9. exercises
10. listened to the radio
11. does the laundry
12. washes the dishes

WORKBOOK PAGE 9

A. FINISH THE SENTENCE

1. c
2. e
3. f
4. g
5. d
6. b
7. a

B. 20 QUESTIONS: *WHAT'S THE OBJECT?*

1. ruler
2. calculator
3. chalk
4. clock
5. map/globe
6. teacher's aide
7. thumbtack
8. graph paper
9. flag
10. seat/chair
11. P.A. system/loudspeaker
12. pencil sharpener
13. desk
14. notebook
15. bookshelf
16. (movie) screen
17. pen
18. eraser
19. eraser
20. computer

WORKBOOK PAGE 10

A. SYNONYMS

1. e
2. a
3. g
4. f
5. h
6. i
7. b
8. d
9. c
10. l
11. o
12. n
13. p
14. j
15. r
16. q
17. k
18. m

B. OPPOSITE ACTIONS

1. Sit down/Take your seat
2. Open
3. Turn, on
4. Take, out
5. passed, out

C. LISTENING

Listen and write the number of the sentence that has the same meaning.

1. Please go over the mistakes.
2. Please hand in the homework.
3. Please take a seat.
4. Please put away the books.
5. Please give out the tests.

Answers

3
5
1
2
4

WORKBOOK PAGE 11

A. WHAT'S THE WORD?

1. Arabic
2. Turkish
3. Sweden, Swedish
4. Spanish, Puerto Rican
5. English, Danish, German, French
6. Vietnamese, Thai, Brazilian, Lebanese
7. Greek, Hebrew, Arabic, Chinese
8. Colombian, Indonesian, Korean, Peruvian

B. LISTENING

Listen and choose the best answer.

1. Anna grew up in New Zealand, where the national language is . . . .
2. The United States Peace Corps sent Bob to Hungary since he speaks . . . .

3. Russian tea is delicious. I had some when I was in . . . .
4. My trip to Costa Rica was wonderful. I had a chance to practice . . . .
5. A Romanian family owns the shop down the street. I was there last week and couldn't understand anything because everybody was speaking . . . .
6. Barbara lived in Brazil for five years. She speaks fluent . . . .
7. My company is opening a branch office in Malaysia, so I've decided to sign up for a course to learn how to speak . . . .
8. I learned to speak Arabic in . . . .
9. Susan is studying Amharic because she's planning to move to . . . .

Answers

1. b	6. b
2. b	7. a
3. a	8. a
4. a	9. a
5. a	

WORKBOOK PAGES 12–13

A. WHAT'S THE WORD?

1. dormitory	6. shelter
2. cabin	7. mobile home
3. single-family house	8. farmhouse
4. condominium	9. nursing home
5. houseboat	

B. ANALOGIES

1. nursing home
2. houseboat
3. townhouse/townhome/duplex/two-family house
4. apartment (building)
5. duplex/two-family house

C. LISTENING: *WHAT ARE THEY TALKING ABOUT?*

Listen and decide what kind of housing these people are talking about.

1. I live on the third floor. My neighbors on the fifth floor are very nice.
2. We like the Watsons very much. We're lucky. After all, their place is attached to ours.
3. We love living here in the country. What a change from the city! Every morning after breakfast we milk the cows.
4. I'm so pleased they put me in Bailey Hall. The rooms are nice, and I'm close to the building where most of my classes are.
5. Mr. Tyler, I know your father will be happy living here. There are many other people his age, and we have a lot of activities I'm sure he'll enjoy.
6. We love living here! We live on the twentieth floor, and the view is fantastic!

Answers

1. a
2. b
3. a
4. b
5. b
6. a

WORKBOOK PAGE 14

A. CAN YOU FIND . . . ?

Things we sit on:	Things that use electricity:	Things to put other things on or in:
armchair	lamp	bookcase
loveseat	stereo system	coffee table
sofa/couch	speaker	end table
	television	mantel
	video cassette recorder/VCR	wall unit/ entertainment unit

Things that are decorative:	Things that reduce light:	Things that are part of the structure of a house:
frame	drapes/curtains	ceiling
painting	lampshade	fireplace
picture/ photograph		floor
plant		wall
rug		window
(throw) pillow		

B. WHICH WORD IS CORRECT?

1. VCR	9. photograph
2. lamp	10. wall
3. drapes	11. mantel
4. painting	12. end table
5. stereo system	13. stereo
6. bookcase	14. unit
7. coffee table	15. fireplace
8. sofa	

WORKBOOK PAGE 15

A. CAN YOU FIND . . . ?

Things that hold cold beverages and foods:	Things that hold hot beverages and foods:	Things that hold food seasonings:
pitcher	china	pepper shaker
salad bowl	coffee pot	salt shaker
serving bowl	serving bowl	
serving platter	serving platter	
china	teapot	
creamer		

Pieces of furniture:	Things used to decorate a table:	Things that give light:
buffet	candle	candle
china cabinet	candlestick	chandelier
(dining room) chair	centerpiece	
(dining room) table	china	
serving cart	tablecloth	

B. WHICH WORD IS CORRECT?

1. platter	8. bowl
2. cabinet	9. buffet
3. centerpiece	10. china cabinet
4. dish	11. chair
5. pitcher	12. sugar bowl/creamer
6. serving cart	13. tablecloth
7. candles	

WORKBOOK PAGE 16

A. TRUE OR FALSE?

1. F	5. F
2. T	6. T
3. F	7. T
4. F	8. F

B. WHAT'S THE WORD?

1. butter knife
2. salad fork
3. knife
4. napkin
5. cup and saucer
6. teaspoon

C. WHICH WORD DOESN'T BELONG?

1. cup (The others are silverware.)
2. butter knife (The others hold liquids.)
3. napkin (The others are dishes.)
4. water glass (The others are silverware.)
5. soup bowl (The others are flat plates.)

D. WHAT'S WRONG WITH THIS PLACE SETTING?

The dinner fork and the salad fork are reversed.
The salad plate and the bread-and-butter plate are reversed.
The napkin is on the wrong side of the plate.
The teaspoon and soup spoon are reversed.
The wine glass and cup and saucer are reversed.

WORKBOOK PAGE 17

A. LISTENING: *FRED'S FURNITURE STORE*

Listen to the following advertisement and write the prices you hear.

For three days, Fred's Furniture Store is having its annual clearance sale. We have fantastic buys on every piece of bedroom furniture in stock. You can buy a twin bed with box spring and mattress for two hundred and ninety-nine dollars! And our famous king-size bed is just three hundred and fifty-nine dollars this week. Yes—just three fifty-nine for our famous king-size bed. And that's not all! Queen-size mattresses with beautiful wooden headboards and footboards are reduced to only three sixty-five. You heard correctly—just three hundred and sixty-five dollars. Also, dressers with mirrors are now on sale for a low three hundred and three dollars. That's right. Just three hundred and three dollars. And finally—the most incredible news of all—every water bed in stock is just two hundred and twenty-five dollars. Just two twenty-five. You'll never see a sale like this again! So come on over to Fred's Furniture Store, at the corner of Pine and Walnut Streets in Lakeville. The sale is for three days only, and its starts today!

Answers

$299 $359 $365 $303 $225

B. WHAT IS IT?

1. alarm clock
2. blinds
3. fitted sheet
4. electric blanket
5. jewelry box
6. pillow
7. bunk bed

C. WHAT'S THE WORD?

1. clock radio
2. mattress
3. flat sheet, fitted sheet
4. queen-size bed, king-size bed

D. WHICH WORD DOESN'T BELONG?

1. blinds (This is the only one that goes on a window.)
2. pillow (The others are used as coverings.)
3. clock radio (The others are pieces of furniture.)
4. electric blanket (The others are beds.)
5. footboard (The others go on top of the bed.)
6. comforter (The others are types of beds.)

WORKBOOK PAGES 18–19

A. CAN YOU FIND . . . ?

Appliances:

dishwasher
(electric) can opener
garbage disposal
microwave (oven)
oven
refrigerator
stove/range
toaster
trash compactor

Cleaning aids:

dishwasher detergent
dishwashing liquid
pot scrubber
scouring pad
sponge

B. LISTENING

Listen and chose the best answer.

1. This garbage is taking up too much room. We'd better use the . . . .
2. The guests will be having a lot of cold drinks. Let's fill up the . . . .

3. Oh, no! What a waste of water! You forgot to turn off the . . . !
4. Let's sit and have a cup of coffee here at the . . . .
5. Ouch! That baking dish was hot! I should have used a . . . .
6. Could you put the shopping list on the refrigerator with this . . . ?
7. To clean that roasting pan you really need a . . . .
8. I found a great recipe in this . . . .
9. It burns everything! I think we need a new . . . .

Answers

1. b
2. a
3. b
4. a
5. b
6. a
7. a
8. a
9. b

C. ANALOGIES

1. paper towel holder
2. sink
3. spice rack
4. freezer
5. refrigerator
6. cutting board
7. scouring pad
8. dishwasher
9. microwave (oven)

D. WHAT'S THE OBJECT?

1. e
2. d
3. b
4. a
5. g
6. c
7. f

E. WHICH WORD DOESN'T BELONG?

1. freezer (The others are hot.)
2. burner (The others are associated with water.)
3. dishwasher detergent (The others are appliances.)
4. kitchen table (The others are containers.)
5. potholder (The others are used for cleaning.)

F. WHAT'S WRONG WITH THIS KITCHEN?

The dishwasher is upside down.
The faucet is on the window.
The microwave oven is sideways.
The toaster is in the freezer.
The paper towels are on the refrigerator.
The canisters are on the stove.
The burners are on the counter.
The garbage is in the middle of the room.
There are dishes in the garbage pail.
The electric can opener is under the sink.
The garbage disposal is on the counter.
The dish towels are in the stove.

WORKBOOK PAGES 20–21

A. EARTHQUAKE!

Small Electrical Appliances:

blender
coffee grinder
coffeemaker
electric frying pan
electric mixer
food processor
griddle
popcorn maker
toaster oven
waffle iron

Bakeware:

cake pan
casserole dish
cookie sheet
mixing bowl
pie plate
rolling pin

Pots and Pans:

cake pan
double boiler
frying pan
lids
pot
pressure cooker
roaster
roasting pan
saucepan
skillet
tea kettle
wok

Small Gadgets and Utensils:

bottle opener
can opener
egg beater
garlic press
grater
ice cream scoop
knife
ladle
measuring cup
measuring spoon
paring knife
spatula
strainer
vegetable peeler
whisk

B. WHICH KITCHENWARE WORD IS CORRECT?

1. spatula
2. strainer
3. grinder
4. rolling pin
5. knife
6. ladle

C. WHAT'S THE OBJECT?

1. b
2. i
3. h
4. c
5. a
6. d
7. e
8. f
9. g

D. WHICH WORD DOESN'T BELONG?

1. ice cream scoop (The others are associated with hot foods.)
2. food processor (The others are used for cooking foods.)
3. double boiler (The others are electric.)
4. garlic press (The others are used for mixing.)
5. saucepan (The others are used for baking.)

E. LISTENING

Listen and choose the best answer.

1. How can we cook these Chinese vegetables?
2. You'll like this brand. It mixes everything very quickly, and it's very quiet.
3. Fill it up with water half-way.
4. I need to peel these apples.
5. It makes all kinds of interesting shapes.
6. I need to cover this pot.

Answers

1. a
2. a
3. a
4. b
5. b
6. a

WORKBOOK PAGES 22–23

A. BABY WORLD

Baby Equipment:	Sleeping Items:	Feeding:
baby carriage	cradle	booster seat
booster seat	crib bumper	food warmer
car seat	portable crib	
diaper pail		
potty		
walker		

Toys:	Furniture:
doll	changing table
stuffed animal	chest of drawers
teddy bear	

B. WHICH WORD IS CORRECT?

1. chest
2. intercom
3. stroller
4. stuffed animal
5. stretch suit
6. car seat

C. CROSSWORD PUZZLE

See page 154.

WORKBOOK PAGE 24

A. DOCTOR'S ADVICE

1. ointment
2. formula
3. disposable diapers
4. pacifier
5. bib
6. diaper pins
7. vitamins
8. cotton swabs

B. ASSOCIATIONS

1. e
2. d
3. b
4. a
5. c

C. LISTENING: *WHAT ARE THEY TALKING ABOUT?*

Listen and decide what's being talked about.

1. They're much more convenient than the cloth ones.
2. I always put one on my baby whenever she eats.
3. It's very gentle and doesn't hurt their eyes.
4. I give them to my child every day. My doctor says they're very important for her health.
5. They're sharp, so be careful when you change the baby!
6. Boy, I wish my mother didn't make me eat this horrible stuff!

Answers

3
2
5
1
6
4

WORKBOOK PAGE 25

A. PROBABLE OR IMPROBABLE?

1. I
2. P
3. P
4. I
5. I
6. P
7. I
8. P
9. I
10. I
11. I

B. WHAT'S THE OBJECT?

1. d
2. a
3. e
4. f
5. b
6. c
7. g

C. WHAT'S THE ACTION?

1. c
2. a
3. e
4. b, d
5. a, d
6. i
7. j
8. h
9. d, g
10. h
11. i
12. f, g
13. i
14. a, k
15. b

WORKBOOK PAGE 26

A. WHAT'S USED WHERE?

1. g
2. d
3. e, f, k, n
4. c
5. a, b
6. o
7. h, i, j, l, m
8. p

B. WHICH WORD IS CORRECT?

1. file
2. polish
3. powder
4. after shave lotion
5. tweezers
6. mascara
7. nail polish remover
8. blade
9. clipper

C. WHICH WORD DOESN'T BELONG?

1. deodorant (The others are used in the mouth.)
2. foundation (The others are used in the hair.)
3. after shave lotion (The others are used while shaving.)
4. styptic pencil (The others are used by women.)
5. tweezers (The others are used on nails.)

D. ANALOGIES

1. shoe polish
2. cologne
3. floss
4. emery board
5. toothpaste

WORKBOOK PAGE 27

A. WHAT DOES NICK NEED?

1. d
2. e
3. p
4. i
5. c, f
6. a
7. j
8. k, m
9. a, c, f, n
10. l
11. h, m
12. b
13. g, n
14. o

B. LISTENING

Listen and choose the best answer.

1. You can hang up these shirts with these . . . .
2. On all my tables I like to use a . . . .
3. I was so upset! The electricity went out when the clothes were in the . . . .
4. Here. Wash these things in the . . . .
5. I always clean my kitchen floor with a . . . .
6. Before I iron my shirts, I use . . . .

Answers

1. a
2. b
3. a
4. b
5. b
6. a

C. ANALOGIES

1. garbage can
2. floor wax
3. clothesline
4. dry mop
5. whisk broom

WORKBOOK PAGES 28–29

A. ASSOCIATIONS

1. d
2. f
3. e
4. a
5. b
6. c

B. WHAT'S THE OBJECT?

1. lamppost
2. antenna
3. lawnmower
4. tool shed
5. shutter
6. barbecue
7. garage
8. drainpipe/downspout
9. storm door
10. doorbell
11. chimney
12. deck, patio

C. WHICH WORD IS CORRECT?

1. roof
2. deck
3. satellite dish
4. storm door
5. screen
6. drainpipe

D. LISTENING: *WHAT ARE THEY TALKING ABOUT?*

Listen and decide what's being talked about.

1. I'm nervous every time someone walks on it. It really needs to be repaved.
2. You should really build a new one. We enjoy ours a lot . . . especially in the warm weather.
3. You're right! They all need to be replaced. Bugs are getting into the house from every window!
4. We love to just sit and relax there every evening after dinner.
5. I agree. It's the best place for the TV antenna.
6. Don't forget to turn it on when we leave tonight!

Answers

1. a
2. b
3. b
4. b
5. a
6. a

E. WHAT'S WRONG WITH THIS HOUSE?

The mailbox is on the roof.
The antenna is on the porch.
The chimney is on the garage.
The garage door is in front of the house.
The doorbell is on the second floor.
There's only one shutter on each window.
The front door is in the garage.
The front walk is in front of the garage.
The lamppost is on top of the garage.

WORKBOOK PAGE 30

MY FIRST APARTMENT

1. swimming pool
2. whirlpool
3. parking garage/parking lot
4. doorman
5. lobby
6. (door) chain/dead-bolt lock
7. dead-bolt lock/(door) chain
8. buzzer
9. intercom
10. peephole
11. elevator
12. laundry room
13. storage room
14. smoke detector
15. air conditioner
16. balcony/terrace
17. superintendent

WORKBOOK PAGES 31-32

A. WHO TO CALL?

1. appliance repair person
2. chimney sweep
3. exterminator
4. carpenter
5. (house) painter
6. handyman
7. locksmith
8. gardener
9. plumber
10. TV repair person

B. LISTENING: *WHAT ARE THEY TALKING ABOUT?*

Listen and decide who or what's being talked about.

1. Eight hundred dollars a month? That's very reasonable.
2. You'd better call Charlie Jones or we won't be able to watch all our favorite programs this weekend.
3. This bill from the exterminator is very high!
4. This is a big bill. I guess we've had a very cold winter.
5. It's very high because we both speak to our parents in Florida every weekend.
6. Uh-oh! Call Patty Anderson. The sink is leaking again!
7. Twenty dollars a month for two cars. That's not too bad.
8. We call Henry Dawson every time we need something done around the house.
9. Who do you use? Your lawn always looks wonderful.
10. We paid a very low price for the house, so our monthly payments aren't very high.
11. I'm calling you because we can't open our front door.

Answers

6	2	9
7	8	3
4	10	11
1	5	

C. PAYING THE BILLS

1. telephone bill
2. water bill
3. electric bill
4. pest control bill
5. heating bill
6. parking fee
7. rent
8. mortgage payment

WORKBOOK PAGE 33

A. CAN YOU FIND . . . ?

Tools for cutting:

hacksaw
hatchet
power saw
saw

Tools and supplies for fastening and unfastening:

bolt
brace
hammer
monkey wrench
nut
Phillips screwdriver
pliers
screw
screwdriver
vise
washer
wrench

Tools for making holes:

(drill) bit
electric drill
hand drill

Tools and equipment for painting:

paint
paintbrush/brush
(paint) pan
(paint) roller
paint thinner
sandpaper
scraper

B. WHICH WORD IS CORRECT?

1. hammer
2. saw
3. bolt, wrench
4. plane
5. scraper
6. vise

C. LISTENING: WHICH TOOL IS IT?

Listen to the sounds. Write the number next to the tool you hear.

1. (Sound: hammer)
2. (Sound: electric drill)
3. (Sound: power saw)
4. (Sound: saw)
5. (Sound: scraper)
6. (Sound: sandpaper)

Answers

3	4
6	1
5	2

WORKBOOK PAGES 34–35

A. ASSOCIATIONS

1. i
2. a
3. e
4. b
5. h
6. g
7. f
8. k
9. c
10. d
11. j

B. WHICH WORD IS CORRECT?

1. flashlight
2. shovel
3. watering can
4. extension cord
5. sprinkler
6. rake
7. hedge clippers
8. garden hose
9. work gloves
10. oil
11. fly swatter
12. grass seed

C. LISTENING: WHAT ARE THEY TALKING ABOUT?

Listen and decide what's being talked about.

1. They're great for trimming our bushes!
2. I cut the grass with it every week!
3. It certainly helps my plants grow!
4. It's the only thing that will catch mice!
5. It's so strong that it'll make these two pieces of wood stick together forever!
6. It'll get rid of all the bugs in your house!

Answers

4
6
1
5
2
3

C. CROSSWORD PUZZLE

See page 154.

WORKBOOK PAGE 36

A. LISTENING: SAME OR DIFFERENT?

As you listen to the following sentences, read the sentences written below. Write S if the sentences are the same or D if the sentences are different.

1. Carol's phone number is three five nine – oh seven eight one.
2. Bill's zip code is four nine two oh nine.
3. Ellen lives at seven fifty-five Massachusetts Avenue.
4. Joseph's office number is area code five oh three, seven five two – eight eight one five.
5. Lisa's social security number is zero zero seven – five two – seven seven six nine.
6. Twelve thousand people were at the baseball game.
7. Chris invited fifty people to his New Year's party.
8. Hal's new Toyota cost forty thousand five hundred eighty-nine dollars.
9. The population of our town is twenty-eight thousand.
10. I just met a person who is fifty-eight but looks eighty!

Answers

1. D
2. S
3. D
4. D
5. S
6. D
7. S
8. D
9. D
10. D

B. ORDINALS

1. fifth
2. second
3. fourth
4. ninetieth
5. fiftieth
6. first
7. twenty-seventh
8. forty-ninth
9. thirty-sixth
10. eighth

C. WHAT'S THE NUMBER?

1. higher
2. my
3. lower
4. fiftieth
5. ninetieth
6. twelfth
7. twenty-one
8. tenth

WORKBOOK PAGE 37

A. ARITHMETIC

1. –
2. ÷
3. ×
4. ×
5. +
6. ÷
7. ×
8. –
9. +

B. LISTENING: FRACTIONS

Listen to the following recipe. Write C if George has put in the correct amount of the ingredients or I if George has put in the incorrect amount.

George is baking banana bread. He's using the following ingredients:

1. two thirds of a cup of sugar
2. a third of a cup of oil
3. two eggs
4. two and a half cups of flour
5. a teaspoon of baking powder
6. three-quarters of a teaspoon of salt

7. a cup and a third of crushed walnuts
8. three ripe bananas

Let's hope your banana bread tastes good, George!

Answers

1. C	5. C
2. I	6. I
3. C	7. I
4. I	8. C

C. PERCENTS

1. $35	6. $750
2. $90	7. $145
3. $27	8. $5.70
4. $120	9. $94.50
5. $14	

WORKBOOK PAGE 38

A. WHAT TIME IS IT?

1. one twenty/twenty after one
2. three forty-five/a quarter to four
3. noon/twelve noon
4. five thirty/half past five
5. midnight/twelve midnight
6. five ten/ten after five
7. eight fifteen/a quarter after eight
8. six fifty/ten to seven
9. twelve forty-five/a quarter to one
10. seven forty/twenty to eight
11. six fifty-five/five to seven
12. five oh five/five after five

B. LISTENING: TRUE OR FALSE?

Listen and write **T** if the sentence is true and **F** if the sentence is false.

1. Joan's train will arrive in New York at twenty after six in the morning.
2. Bob and Betsy arrived for lunch at noon.
3. Sharon had to wait until a quarter after five to see Dr. Block.
4. David went to bed at ten to eleven.
5. Walter's bus will get in from Denver at two thirty-eight in the afternoon.
6. John has an appointment to see Professor Cates at ten minutes to four.
7. Margaret babysat from ten in the morning until half past eleven at night.

Answers

1. T	5. T
2. T	6. F
3. F	7. T
4. T	

WORKBOOK PAGE 39

A. U.S. CALENDAR QUIZ

1. April	6. September
2. February	7. April, May
3. fourth, July	8. June
4. January	9. Monday
5. Saturday	10. November

WORKBOOK PAGES 40–41

A. WHERE CAN I GET . . . ?

1. clothing store/department store/discount store
2. auto dealer/car dealer/gas station/service station
3. barber shop/hair salon
4. travel agency
5. drug store/pharmacy
6. gas station/service station
7. clothing store/department store/discount store/ shoe store/shopping mall
8. convenience store/grocery store/supermarket
9. department store/discount store/ hardware store/supermarket
10. bakery/ice cream shop/supermarket
11. cafeteria/coffee shop/delicatessen/deli/hotel
12. pet shop
13. flower shop/florist/supermarket
14. health club/spa
15. toy store/department store/discount store
16. cafeteria/ice cream shop/restaurant
17. book store/library
18. clinic/hospital
19. vision center/eyeglass store
20. cleaners/dry cleaners
21. restaurant
22. health club/spa/hotel
23. barber shop
24. bus station/train station
25. post office
26. jewelry store/department store/discount store
27. computer store/discount store
28. appliance store/hardware store/department store/ discount store
29. cafeteria/donut shop/coffee shop/pizza shop/restaurant
30. bank

B. WHERE CAN I . . . ?

1. concert hall
2. movie theater
3. park
4. museum
5. zoo
6. park
7. photo shop/supermarket/pharmacy
8. laundromat
9. maternity shop/department store/discount store
10. video store/supermarket

C. WHICH WORD DOESN'T BELONG?

1. park (The others are associated with cars.)
2. barber shop (The others are associated with food.)
3. copy center (The others are associated with music.)
4. convenience store (The others are all places where you sleep.)
5. drug store (The others all have *screens*.)
6. photo shop (The others are all *stations*.)
7. hair salon (The others are associated with clothing.)
8. coffee shop (The others are associated with children.)
9. vision center (The others are associated with travel.)
10. shoe store (The others are all places where your drop things, or people, off.)

D. ANALOGIES

1. donut shop	6. museum
2. pet shop	7. concert hall
3. video store	8. motel
4. health club	9. laundromat
5. parking lot/parking garage	

WORKBOOK PAGE 42

WHAT'S THE WORD?

1. fire alarm
2. meter maid, parking meter
3. taxi stand
4. street light
5. pedestrian, crosswalk
6. newsstand
7. bench
8. garbage truck
9. drive-through window
10. curb
11. courthouse

12. phone booth/public telephone
13. street sign, street
14. office building
15. trash container

WORKBOOK PAGES 43–44

A. WHAT'S THE CATEGORY?

1. f	6. a
2. d	7. c
3. e	8. i
4. j	9. g
5. h	10. b

B. THE RIGHT WORD

1. fast	7. dry
2. soft	8. clean
3. low	9. full
4. loud	10. high
5. difficult	11. hot
6. thick	12. bad

C. SYNONYMS

1. l	9. i
2. e	10. b
3. h	11. h
4. d	12. f
5. a	13. c
6. k	14. j
7. b	15. e
8. k	

D. "SKY HIGH!"

1. sky	7. filthy
2. dirt	8. boiling
3. ice	9. brand
4. pitch	10. razor
5. bone	11. sparkling
6. chock	12. skin

E. LISTENING

Listen and choose the best answer.

1. After Larry's diet, all his pants were too . . . .
2. The dentist has recommended braces for Timmy because his teeth are . . . .
3. I can't possibly fit through this doorway! It's too . . . .
4. That's strange. I thought I had locked the door, but when I returned home I found it . . . .
5. Watch out! Those new knives are really . . . !
6. Carol's hair takes a long time to dry because it's so . . . .
7. That new furniture polish works very well. Our table looks so . . . !
8. This car gets excellent mileage. After driving a few hours, the tank is almost . . . !
9. This dryer must be broken. All the clothes are still . . . !
10. I don't understand it. I've been boiling these eggs for twenty minutes and they're still . . . !
11. Although Jan prepared for the TOEFL exam, she still found it quite . . . .
12. Because medical technology enables people to live longer, a large percentage of the population is . . . .

Answers

1. a	7. a
2. b	8. b
3. b	9. a
4. a	10. b
5. a	11. b
6. b	12. b

WORKBOOK PAGES 45–46

A. WHICH WORD DOESN'T BELONG?

1. shocked (The others are *happy* words.)
2. proud (The others are *tired* words.)
3. nervous (The others are *angry* words.)
4. bored (The others are *upset* words.)
5. jealous (The others are *eating* or *drinking* words.)

B. ANALOGIES

1. exhausted	4. proud
2. afraid	5. shocked
3. disappointed	

C. THE NEXT WORD

1. b, c, e	4. b, d, e
2. a, b	5. b, c, d
3. b	

D. SYNONYMS

1. d	5. h
2. f	6. a
3. c	7. e
4. g	8. b

E. WHICH WORD IS CORRECT?

1. exhausted	6. sick
2. frustrated	7. shocked
3. full	8. miserable
4. confused	9. embarrassed
5. proud	

F. LISTENING: *HOW ARE THEY FEELING?*

Listen and choose the best description of the person's feelings.

1. I didn't sleep at all last night!
2. I can't believe it! Someone banged into my new car!
3. My dentist took out a tooth last Friday, and I couldn't eat or sleep all weekend.
4. I've got a fever, my head is congested, and my nose is running.
5. I didn't get the promotion I was expecting.
6. My wife just had twin boys!
7. I have an important English exam tomorrow.
8. I have no idea what I'm going to do when I finish school.

Answers

1. a	5. a
2. b	6. b
3. a	7. b
4. b	8. a

G. "FREEZING COLD!"

1. d	6. g
2. e	7. h
3. c	8. f
4. a	9. j
5. b	10. i

WORKBOOK PAGE 47

A. WHAT'S THE FRUIT?

1. c	6. g
2. f	7. d
3. e	8. i
4. a	9. h
5. j	10. b

B. WHICH FRUIT?

1. orange	4. grapes
2. blueberry	5. tangerine
3. banana	6. watermelon

C. "THE APPLE OF MY EYE!"

1. b	4. b
2. a	5. a
3. b	6. a

WORKBOOK PAGE 48

A. TOSSED SALAD!

1. lettuce
2. celery
3. cucumber
4. tomato
5. radish
6. scallions
7. red pepper
8. artichoke
9. mushrooms

B. WHICH VEGETABLE DOESN'T BELONG?

1. turnip (The others are green vegetables.)
2. brussels sprout (The others are long vegetables.)
3. tomato (The others are white vegetables.)
4. asparagus (The others are yellow vegetables.)
5. kidney (The others are kinds of onions.)
6. beet (The others are kinds of beans.)
7. cucumber (The others come in a *head*.)

C. TRUE OR FALSE?

1. T
2. F
3. F
4. T
5. T
6. T
7. F
8. F

D. CAN YOU REMBEMBER?

Squash:	Peppers:	Onions:	Beans:
zucchini	red	green	string/green
acorn	green	red	lima
butternut	pearl	black
			kidney

WORKBOOK PAGES 49–50

A. CATEGORIES

1. sour: milk/dairy products
2. chops: poultry
3. halibut: juice
4. paks: shellfish
5. lemonade: dairy products
6. frozen dinners: canned goods
7. soup: beverages
8. cake: bread
9. shrimp: meat
10. duck: fish
11. scallops: packaged goods
12. seafood: things to drink
13. roast: poultry
14. soup: juice

B. WHAT'S THE FOOD?

1. d
2. j
3. o
4. m
5. g
6. d
7. a
8. c
9. p
10. h
11. b
12. e
13. l
14. f
15. i
16. k

C. WHAT SHOULD I DO?

1. b
2. c
3. d
4. a

D. WHICH WORD IS CORRECT?

1. mussels
2. lamb
3. chicken
4. frozen vegetables
5. trout
6. spaghetti
7. powdered drink mix
8. chicken
9. Orange juice
10. skim milk
11. pita

WORKBOOK PAGES 51–52

A. LIKELY OR UNLIKELY?

	Likely	Unlikely
1.		✔
2.	✔	
3.	✔	
4.		✔
5.		✔
6.		✔
7.		✔
8.	✔	
9.		✔

B. LISTENING

Listen and choose the best answer.

1. I'd like some roast . . . .
2. Please hand me the nacho . . . .
3. I only drink decaf . . . .
4. Excuse me. Where are the baby . . . ?
5. I love soy . . . .
6. I'm looking for the waxed . . . .
7. We need to buy some plastic . . . .
8. We're having a special on macaroni . . . .
9. We're almost out of dog . . . .
10. I can't find the cake . . . .
11. Excuse me. Are you using this shopping . . . ?
12. I'm looking for Household . . . .

Answers

1. a
2. b
3. b
4. b
5. b
6. a
7. b
8. a
9. b
10. a
11. b
12. b

C. WORD SEARCH

S	H	O	P	E	R	K	E	R	N	X	F	M	O
C	T	L	A	L	U	M	I	N	U	M	F	O	I	L
A	K	O	L	A	J	G	F	M	O	N	L	D	H	B
L	E	H	T	S	P	U	R	J	T	B	X	P	L	T
E	G	D	C	T	N	D	I	A	P	E	R	S	P	Q
P	I	O	V	I	F	M	D	I	T	W	Q	T	B	N
T	A	G	A	C	C	S	P	R	F	X	C	R	I	F
I	I	F	G	W	I	P	E	S	Z	C	Z	A	A	L
C	S	O	U	R	Q	H	O	I	U	V	N	W	S	O
B	L	O	E	A	Z	N	L	Y	S	X	F	S	W	N
H	E	D	F	P	X	C	A	R	T	P	W	S	D	E

D. "BREAD AND BUTTER"

1. butter
2. cheese
3. vinegar
4. bacon
5. pepper
6. mustard

E. WHICH WORD DOESN'T BELONG?

1. pickles (The others are deli meats.)
2. macaroni (The others are types of cheese.)
3. cole (The others are kinds of chips.)
4. straws (The others are baby items.)
5. scanner (The others are people.)
6. salami (The others are types of salad.)
7. jelly (The others are condiments.)

8. food (The others are paper products.)
9. candy (The others are related to paying for items.)
10. decaf (The others are categories of foods.)

F. ASSOCIATIONS

1. f	8. m
2. k	9. e
3. l	10. c
4. b	11. g
5. a	12. d
6. h	13. i
7. n	14. j

WORKBOOK PAGE 53

A. WHICH WORD IS CORRECT?

1. bar	7. jar, bottle
2. bunch	8. bottle
3. ears	9. tube
4. six-pack	10. loaves
5. pack	11. packages, rolls
6. sticks	12. box

B. LISTENING: *WHAT ARE THEY TALKING ABOUT?*
Listen and decide what's being talked about.
1. I bought a can the other day.
2. Pick up a liter bottle when you go to the store.
3. Careful! That box is going to fall off the table!
4. You can get four jars for two dollars.
5. I ate five ears!
6. We really could use one or two heads.
7. Could you pick up a pint when you're at the supermarket?
8. You used up the whole package?!
9. I think there's a bar in the bathroom.
Answers

1. a	6. a
2. a	7. a
3. a	8. a
4. b	9. b
5. b	

C. LISTENING: *WHAT'S THE CONTAINER?*
Listen and choose the correct container or quantity.

1.	butter	cheese	beef
2.	sugar	flour	chips
3.	toilet tissue	plastic wrap	paper towels
4.	cereal	cookies	raisins
5.	tomatoes	tuna fish	soup
6.	grapes	carrots	bananas
7.	eggs	milk	orange juice
8.	yogurt	cottage cheese	sour cream

Answers

4	6
2	7
5	8
1	3

WORKBOOK PAGE 54

A. TRUE OR FALSE?

1. T	7. T
2. F	8. F
3. F	9. F
4. T	10. T
5. F	11. F
6. T	12. F

B. FIGURE IT OUT!

1. 2 cups	4. 2 quarts
2. 2 teaspoons	5. 2 pounds
3. 1/2 cup	6. 1/4 lb., 1/2 lb.

WORKBOOK PAGE 55

A. HELP!

1. d	5. b
2. f	6. h
3. a	7. c
4. g	8. e

B. LISTENING: *WHAT ARE THEY TALKING ABOUT?*
Listen and decide what's being talked about.
1. I've already peeled them.
2. How long should I stir it?
3. The directions on the box say to boil it for five minutes.
4. I think I'll saute it.
5. I like them scrambled.
6. We had them boiled the other day. I think I'll broil them tonight.
Answers

1. a	4. b
2. a	5. a
3. b	6. b

C. LISTENING: *WHAT'S THE CATEGORY?*
Listen and choose the appropriate category.

1.	milk	juice	lemonade
2.	cheese	carrots	onions
3.	eggs	celery	lettuce
4.	turkey	roast beef	leg of lamb
5.	steak	hot dogs	hamburgers
6.	cake	rolls	bread

Answers

4	1	2
3	6	5

WORKBOOK PAGE 56

A. WHAT'S THE FOOD?

1. g	7. j
2. e	8. a
3. k	9. i
4. c	10. d
5. h	11. l
6. f	12. b

B. WHAT'S FOR BREAKFAST?

donut	danish
muffin	croissant
bagel	biscuit
coffee	

C. LISTENING: *WHAT FOOD ARE THEY TALKING ABOUT?*
Listen and decide what food is being talked about.
1. A. Do you have the ingredients?
   B. I think so. I've got the meat, the cheese, and the lettuce.
2. A. Do you like it with cream and sugar?
   B. Yes, please.
3. A. I'm trying to lose weight.
   B. Then I know what you should have to drink.
4. A. Is it greasy?
   B. Yes. It's a little greasy.
5. A. How many slices should I put in the sandwich?
   B. Three or four.
6. A. This tastes delicious. What's the secret of your recipe?
   B. I use lots of spices.
Answers

1. a	4. b
2. b	5. b
3. a	6. a

WORKBOOK PAGE 57

A. AT THE RIVERSIDE RESTAURANT

<u>6</u>
<u>7</u>
<u>2</u>
<u>9</u>
<u>1</u>
<u>4</u>
<u>10</u>
<u>8</u>
<u>3</u>
<u>5</u>

B. FOOD TALK!

1. tasty
2. Crisp
3. weren't
4. out of this world
5. fresh
6. never
7. aren't
8. sweet
9. soggy
10. raw
11. wonderful
12. warm

WORKBOOK PAGE 58

A. COLOR ASSOCIATIONS

1. yellow
2. red
3. white
4. green, black
5. green
6. blue
7. red
8. yellow
9. purple
10. orange

B. MIXING COLORS

1. pink
2. orange
3. green
4. purple
5. gray
6. brown

C. COLORFUL EXPRESSIONS!

1. red
2. blue
3. gray
4. black
5. green
6. blue
7. Blue
8. yellow
9. white
10. black
11. pink, green
12. white
13. yellow
14. white

WORKBOOK PAGE 59

A. WHO WEARS WHAT?

1. W
2. B
3. B
4. M
5. B
6. B
7. B
8. W
9. W
10. M
11. M
12. M
13. B
14. M
15. W

B. WHAT TO WEAR?

1. d, h, i
2. b, p
3. f
4. e, h, i, j, m
5. c, m, n, o
6. l
7. a, g, k, p

C. LISTENING

Listen and choose the best answer.
1. The weather is going to be cool. You'd better wear your . . . .
2. If you wear that skirt, I think you should wear this green . . . .
3. I really like my new suit. To go with it, I think I'll buy myself a new . . . .
4. I love your new V-neck . . . !

5. Since Tom's party is going to be very informal, I think I'll wear my new black . . . .
6. When it's warm out, I always wear a . . . .
Answers
1. b
2. a
3. b
4. a
5. a
6. b

WORKBOOK PAGE 60

A. WHAT KIND OF SHOES DO THEY NEED?

1. a, g
2. b
3. j, l
4. f, i
5. h
6. d, k
7. j
8. c

B. LISTENING: *WHAT'S BEING DESCRIBED?*

Listen and decide what's being described.
1. Many men put these on before they go to bed.
2. You put it on after a shower or before you get dressed in the morning. It's often thick and made of a fabric called terry cloth. White ones are very common.
3. This is often worn by men and boys under their shirts. This article of clothing is usually white and made of soft cotton.
4. People wear them on their feet before they get dressed in the morning or after a bath. People don't usually wear them outside the home.
5. Many men wear these underneath their pants. They usually come in many colors and patterns.
6. In winter, many people wear these under their slacks and jeans to keep warm. In fact, I'm going skiing next weekend, and I want to take along a pair of these with me.

Answers

<u>4</u> <u>5</u>
<u>6</u> <u>1</u>
<u>2</u> <u>3</u>

C. LISTENING

Listen and choose the best answer.
1. I'm ready for the marathon with my new . . . .
2. I have a job interview today. I think I'll wear my blue suit and my matching . . . .
3. For Bob's birthday I think I'll buy him new . . . .
4. I really like this black skirt. To wear under it, I think I'll buy a new . . . .
5. When I exercise, I always wear good . . . .
6. My son is going to college next week. I need to buy him several pairs of . . . .
7. Helen just bought a beautiful new party dress. To go with it, she plans to buy a pair of . . . .
8. It's raining. Don't forget to wear your . . . !
9. When my brother and I play sports, we always wear . . . .
Answers
1. b
2. a
3. a
4. a
5. b
6. b
7. a
8. b
9. a

WORKBOOK PAGES 61–62

A. WHICH WORD DOESN'T BELONG?

1. overcoat (The others are worn in the rain.)
2. tank top (The others are worn on the head.)
3. sweat (The others are types of shorts.)
4. jacket (The others are worn on the head.)
5. windbreaker (The others are worn for exercising.)

B. WHICH WOULDN'T YOU WEAR?

1. trenchcoat
   rubbers
   leotard

2. lycra shorts
3. tee shirt
   overcoat
   tank top
4. rubbers
   ski mask
5. bomber jacket
   down jacket
   scarf
6. ear muffs
   rain hat
   beret
   mittens

C. A LETTER FROM SEATTLE

1. raincoat
2. rubbers
3. windbreaker
4. jacket, vest
5. vest, jacket
6. gloves, mittens
7. mittens, gloves
8. scarf
9. hat
10. earmuffs

WORKBOOK PAGE 63

A. CAN YOU FIND . . . ?

Items that go around your neck:

beads
chain
necklace
pearls

Items that can be used to carry things:

backpack
book bag
briefcase
purse/pocketbook/ handbag
shoulder bag
tote bag

Accessories ususally worn with shirts, pants, and ties:

cufflinks
tie pin/tie tack
tie clip
belt

Pieces of jewelry that can be worn on the wrist:

bracelet
watch

B. LIKELY OR UNLIKELY?

	Likely	Unlikely
1.	✔	
2.		✔
3.		✔
4.		✔
5.	✔	
6.		✔
7.	✔	
8.	✔	
9.		✔
10.		✔
11.		✔

C. LISTENING: WHAT IS IT?

Listen and decide what's being described.

1. It's for carrying coins.
2. It holds your pants or skirt up.
3. It's for carrying school texts.
4. Business executives carry their important papers in it.
5. It's usually plain gold, and people in the U.S. wear it on their left hand.
6. They're white and beautiful. They're a popular gift for women.
7. It's what the future groom gives to the future bride.
8. You take it with you when you go camping.

Answers

4	2	7	1
6	8	3	5

WORKBOOK PAGE 64

A. WHAT'S THE WORD?

1. long
2. lower
3. print
4. looser
5. heavier
6. narrower

B. LISTENING: THE FASHION SHOW

Match the description you hear with the appropriate design.

1. Angela is ready for a party in this exciting print gown.
2. This season, polka dots are back in style.
3. Laura looks festive in a red and green plaid suit.
4. Paisley is always a good choice for all, as Marie demonstrates.
5. Tammy looks like spring in this flowered skirt and blouse.
6. And Julie is wearing a lovely multicolored striped dress.
7. Tony shows how attractive that checked shirt can look with the right accessories.
8. For that elegant dinner, Mark is wearing solid black.

Answers

3	6	5	1
4	8	2	7

C. LISTENING: WEDDING GOSSIP

Listen and complete each nasty sentence of this couple gossiping at a family wedding.

A. Just look at Agnes! For such a formal wedding, her dress is much too . . . !
B. And will you look at Cousin Millie's shoes! How can she dance? The heels on her shoes are so . . . !
A. My! My! Look at Uncle Wally! He's put on a few pounds and that suit of his is VERY . . . !
B. And Aunt Esther! It's absolutely disgraceful! Her skirt is so . . . !
A. Don't you think for such a hot summer day Louise's dress is awfully . . . ?
B. Yes, I do. And look at Ellie! She can hardly walk! She has such wide feet, and she insists on wearing shoes that are too . . . !
A. And Uncle Jake! You'd think he was going to a funeral instead of a wedding. His suit is so . . . !
B. I'm having a marvelous time. It's so nice being with family members, isn't it?
A. It certainly is.

Answers

1. a
2. a
3. b
4. b
5. a
6. a
7. a

WORKBOOK PAGE 65

A. GOING SHOPPING

1. Men's Clothing
2. Jewelry
3. Electronics
4. Children's Clothing
5. Furniture/Home Furnishings
6. Housewares
7. Women's Clothing
8. Household Appliances
9. Perfume

B. LISTENING: *ATTENTION SHOPPERS!*

Match the following announcements to the appropriate department.

1. Children's overalls and matching jerseys are now on sale! Get them while they last!
2. Get that someone special a diamond ring this holiday season!
3. Need a new washer and dryer? Now's the time to get them at reasonable prices!
4. Blenders, mixers, food processors—to serve all your baking needs!
5. Hear the latest hits on top-of-the-line equipment—CD players, cassette players, and speakers—all at affordable prices!
6. New designer ties at low, low prices! This week only!
7. Colognes, perfumes, and lotions from all the well-known manufacturers available here!
8. Suits and dresses for work and play from leading designers! For the best selection, hurry over now!
9. Matching beds, dressers, and night tables! Prices dramatically reduced!

Answers

9	8	6
3	7	4
1	5	2

C. HELP ME!

1. d
2. e
3. a
4. b
5. c
6. f

D. LISTENING: *WHERE ARE THEY?*

Listen and decide in which departments or areas of a department store you would most likely hear the following conversations.

1. A. Where can I find toasters?
   B. I'm sorry, but we're all out.

2. A. Would you please push "five"?
   B. Certainly.

3. A. This is moving so slowly!
   B. We should have taken the elevator.

4. A. Where can I try these on?
   B. There's a dressing room over there, ma'am.

5. A. Look at that dress over there!
   B. Can I have it? It's just like yours, Mommy!

6. A. You'd like to return this?
   B. Yes, I would.
   A. Do you have the receipt?
   B. Yes. Here it is.

7. A. Do you have Christmas wrapping paper?
   B. Yes, we do.

8. A. Can I help you?
   B. Yes, I'd like a cup of coffee.

9. A. Which floor did we leave the car on?
   B. The second, I think.

Answers

6	1	3
8	2	7
9	5	4

WORKBOOK PAGE 66

A. WHAT AM I?

1. record player
2. camcorder
3. blank videotape
4. set of headphones
5. TV
6. VCR
7. speaker
8. Walkman
9. alarm clock
10. shortwave radio

B. LISTENING: *A SALE AT TECH HI-FI*

Listen to the commercial and fill in the correct information.

Ring in the New Year with the annual New Year's Sale at Tech Hi-Fi! Come take advantage of unbelievable savings before it's too late. Sony eight-inch screen TVs with remote control—twenty percent off. Camcorders and VCRs—up to fifty percent off. And don't forget to stock up on blank videotapes while you're here. Get four blank videotapes for only ten dollars. Listen to your favorite tunes on quality equipment. Prices on turntables, tape decks, and CD players have all been slashed from ten to sixty percent. And for those of you on the go, buy a portable radio cassette player or Walkman and save up to seventy-five percent on famous brands. Name-brand radios—clock, shortwave, and portable—some selling for as low as twenty-five dollars. Hurry! Come to Tech Hi-Fi while supplies last!

Answers

1. 20
2. 50
3. 10
4. 10, 60
5. 75
6. 25

WORKBOOK PAGE 67

A. CROSSWORD PUZZLE

See page 155.

B. LISTENING

Listen and choose the best answer.

1. I'd like to get a close-up of that rare bird. Where's my . . . ?
2. "Please leave a message after the beep" is the recording often heard on . . . .
3. In the field of language teaching, people are developing some very interesting . . . .
4. Most office work is done on computers nowadays, but previously people used . . . .
5. If you like to do chores while talking, you should really buy a . . . .
6. I knew we were in for a long boring evening when the Johnsons took out their . . . .
7. If you want to take pictures of Billy's birthday party, don't forget to use the . . . .
8. I never add, subtract, multiply, or divide by myself any more. I use a . . . .
9. The *s* and the *t* are stuck! I really need to fix my . . . !

Answers

1. a
2. b
3. a
4. b
5. b
6. a
7. a
8. b
9. b

WORKBOOK PAGE 68

A. WHICH TOY DOESN'T BELONG?

1. bicycle (The others are miniature.)
2. doll house (The others are for use outdoors.)
3. coloring book (The others are implements used for drawing or painting.)
4. toy truck (The others are replicas of people or animals.)
5. trading cards (The others are round.)
6. swing set (The others have wheels.)

B. A LETTER TO SANTA

1. doll house
2. doll house furniture
3. hula hoop
4. bubble soap
5. walkie-talkie (set)
6. science kit
7. pail/shovel
8. shovel/pail
9. beach ball
10. crayons/color markers
11. color markers/crayons
12. paint set

WORKBOOK PAGE 69

A. LISTENING

Listen and write the amount of money you hear.

1. For my mother's birthday, I bought her a blouse for nineteen fifty.
2. Here. Your change is thirteen dollars and sixty-three cents.
3. You know, there are still some places where you can get a sandwich and a drink for a dollar twenty-five.
4. This camera isn't very expensive. It's only seventy-seven dollars and eighty-nine cents.
5. All right, you can have one piece of candy. Here's seven cents.
6. The taxi ride to the airport cost me over nineteen dollars.
7. With the tax, that comes to two hundred and forty-nine dollars and thirty-eight cents.
8. Look! It's on sale for only ninety-nine ninety-nine!
9. I don't care if they say it's an antique! I wouldn't pay one cent for this old piece of junk!

Answers

1. $19.50
2. $13.63
3. $1.25
4. $77.89
5. $.07/7¢
6. $19.00
7. $249.38
8. $99.99
9. $.01/1¢

B. HOW MUCH DO THEY COST?

1. c
2. b
3. a
4. f
5. d
6. e

C. ANOTHER WAY OF SAYING IT

1. ten cents
2. five cents
3. one cent
4. a dollar
5. thousand

D. GETTING CHANGE

1. $1.15
2. $6.00
3. $.25/25¢
4. $.05/5¢
5. $10.00
6. $.84/84¢

WORKBOOK PAGE 70

A. BANK TALK

1. slip
2. card
3. order
4. statement
5. application
6. book
7. register

B. LIKELY OR UNLIKELY?

	Likely	Unlikely
1.		✔
2.		✔
3.		✔
4.	✔	
5.		✔
6.		✔

C. LISTENING: *THE BANK ROBBERY*

Listen and decide whether the following statements are true or false.

Yesterday afternoon an attempted robbery took place at the State Street Bank. A robber approached one of the tellers and demanded that he open the bank vault. The teller called the bank officer who had the combination to the vault and she opened it. The robber ordered the teller and the bank officer to put one million dollars in cash as well as the contents of the safe deposit boxes into a bag. Fortunately, the security guard who had been in the lobby where the ATM machines are located managed to set off the silent alarm and the police came and intercepted the robber.

Answers

1. T
2. T
3. F
4. F
5. T

WORKBOOK PAGES 71–72

A. WHICH WORD DOESN'T BELONG?

1. eyelid (The others have hair.)
2. chin (The others are below the waist.)
3. wrist (The others are fingers.)
4. knuckle (The others are part of the foot.)
5. temple (The others are part of the eye.)
6. lip (The others are internal parts of the body.)
7. veins (The others are organs.)
8. calf (The others are part of the hand.)

B. WHICH WORD IS CORRECT?

1. ankle
2. jaw
3. waist
4. cornea
5. forehead
6. back
7. stomach
8. pinky
9. nose
10. heart
11. shin
12. shoulder
13. abdomen
14. gall bladder
15. arm

C. WHAT'S THE ACTION?

1. d
2. q
3. n
4. j
5. a
6. o
7. b
8. l
9. g
10. r
11. p
12. i
13. e
14. m
15. h
16. c
17. k
18. f
19. s

D. "PUT YOUR BEST FOOT FORWARD!"

1. foot
2. tongue
3. face, face
4. nose
5. cheek, cheek
6. chin
7. chest
8. elbow
9. heart
10. back
11. skin, bone
12. thumb
13. neck, neck
14. shoulder
15. stomach
16. leg

WORKBOOK PAGES 73–74

A. WHAT'S AILING THEM?

1. a
2. b
3. b
4. b
5. a
6. b
7. a
8. b
9. a
10. b
11. a

B. ABSOLUTELY MISERABLE!

1. hurt
2. wrist
3. ankle
4. knee
5. cornea
6. hip
7. virus
8. congested
9. bloated
10. neck

C. OH, MY ACHING BACK!

1. aching
2. high
3. scratchy
4. upset
5. hacking
6. pounding
7. itchy

WORKBOOK PAGE 75

A. WHAT'S THE WORD?

1. optometrist
2. dentist
3. cardiologist
4. pediatrician
5. obstetrician
6. scale, examination table, stethoscope
7. psychiatrist
8. surgeon
9. thermometer, needle

B. LISTENING: *WHERE ARE THEY?*

Listen and decide where these people are.

1. I need to weigh you and take your blood pressure.
2. Please sit still while I take a picture of your lungs.
3. Don't worry. We'll be at the hospital in just a few minutes.
4. Can you see the eye chart?
5. Lie down and tell me all the thoughts that come into your head.
6. Next! Tell me your name and the problem you're having.
7. Now I'm going to give you a shot of Novacaine.
8. I'll have this liver repaired in just a few minutes.

Answers

6
2
5
1
4
8
3
7

WORKBOOK PAGE 76

A. A GOOD IDEA!/NOT A GOOD IDEA!

	A Good Idea	Not a Good Idea
1.	✔	
2.	✔	
3.		✔
4.		✔
5.		✔
6.	✔	
7.	✔	
8.		✔
9.	✔	
10.		✔
11.	✔	
12.		✔

B. LISTENING: *WHAT ARE THEY TALKING ABOUT?*

Listen and decide what's being talked about.

1. Walk about a mile every day and you'll feel better.
2. You'll wear this while you're a patient here.
3. I'm afraid this bad cut won't heal without them.
4. Read this and you'll see what medications this patient is taking.
5. Remember. Do it three times a day with salt water.
6. Once we remove your gall bladder, you'll feel much better.
7. Just push it and a nurse will come right in.
8. These pictures will show how serious the problem is.
9. You'll need this since you won't be able to walk to the bathroom.
10. Your medication will drip through this very slowly.

Answers

6	8
3	2
5	7
10	1
4	9

C. ASSOCIATIONS

1. d
2. g
3. f
4. h
5. b
6. a
7. c
8. e

WORKBOOK PAGE 77

A. AILMENTS AND REMEDIES

1. aspirin, ice pack
2. cough syrup, cough drops
3. throat lozenges
4. vitamins
5. eye drops
6. aspirin, ointment, creme, heating pad
7. ointment, cream, lotion
8. aspirin, cold tablets, throat lozenges, decongestant spray/nasal spray
9. decongestant spray/nasal spray
10. ice pack
11. throat lozenges
12. wheelchair

B. INTERNAL OR EXTERNAL?

1. I
2. I
3. E
4. I
5. E
6. I
7. I
8. E
9. I

C. TAKE OR USE?

1. take
2. use
3. use
4. use
5. took
6. take

WORKBOOK PAGE 78

A. WHICH WORD IS CORRECT?

1. zip code
2. letter
3. letter
4. money order
5. change-of-address
6. window
7. express mail
8. registered
9. return address
10. mail slot
11. postcard
12. mail bag
13. book rate
14. address
15. roll of stamps
16. airmail
17. stamp machine
18. selective service
19. postal clerk

B. LISTENING

Listen and choose the best answer.

1. Step over here to the next . . . .
2. I'd like to buy a . . . .
3. He's our new . . . .
4. I'd like to send this first . . . .
5. I don't want a sheet of stamps. I'd prefer a . . . .
6. You can buy stamps over there in the . . . .

Answers

1. b
2. a
3. b
4. b
5. a
6. b

WORKBOOK PAGES 79–80

A. THE MIDVILLE LIBRARY

1. librarian
2. card catalog
3. author
4. title
5. call card
6. call number
7. shelves
8. checkout desk
9. library assistant
10. reference section
11. dictionary
12. encyclopedia
13. atlas
14. reference librarian
15. periodicals section
16. newspaper
17. magazine
18. photocopy machine
19. media section
20. record/tape
21. tape/record
22. videotape
23. microfiche
24. microfilm

B. LISTENING: *WHAT ARE THEY TALKING ABOUT?*

Listen and decide what's being talked about.

1. If you lose it, you won't be able to take books out of the library.
2. It has all the major newspapers from around the world.
3. It tells you the author's name as well as the title and subject of the book.
4. I'm fascinated by geography. That's why I love to look through one whenever I have the time.
5. It has a computerized listing of all the books in the library.
6. It has all the information about the world you would ever need to know.
7. I'd like to find a good bilingual one with definitions I can understand.
8. This is where we keep all our records and tapes.
9. Remember! You need to stop here on your way out of the library if you're checking out a book.

Answers

6	8	7
3	9	4
5	2	1

C. LIKELY OR UNLIKELY?

	Likely	Unlikely
1.	✔	
2.		✔
3.	✔	
4.		✔
5.		✔
6.	✔	
7.	✔	
8.		✔
9.		✔
10.	✔	
11.		✔

WORKBOOK PAGE 81

A. WHAT'S THE WORD?

1. office
2. auditorium
3. (school) nurse
4. track
5. teacher, language lab
6. driver's ed instructor
7. teachers' lounge
8. coach
9. guidance counselor
10. assistant principal
11. custodian
12. locker room, gym/gymnasium

B. LISTENING: *WHO'S TALKING?*

Listen and decide who is talking.

1. As we discussed at our last meeting, I think you should take physics next semester.
2. Is it okay to clean in here?
3. As head of the school, I am pleased to welcome you all to Midville High.
4. I want you to report for practice right after classes end.
5. When you finish the test, you can have lunch.
6. Next! What would you like to have?

Answers

1. a	4. b
2. a	5. a
3. a	6. b

WORKBOOK PAGES 82–83

A. A LETTER HOME

1. biology
2. geography
3. Spanish
4. industrial arts/shop
5. home economics
6. choir/chorus
7. drama
8. student government
9. literary magazine
10. football

B. WHICH COURSE?

1. d	6. i
2. h	7. e
3. a	8. b
4. f	9. g
5. c	

C. ASSOCIATIONS

1. d	4. e
2. f	5. c
3. a	6. b

D. LIKELY OR UNLIKELY?

	Likely	Unlikely
1.	✔	
2.		✔
3.		✔
4.	✔	
5.		✔
6.	✔	
7.		✔

WORKBOOK PAGES 84–85

A. WHAT'S THE OCCUPATION?

1. secretary
2. journalist
3. accountant
4. waitress
5. architect
6. translator
7. baker
8. lawyer
9. chef
10. pharmacist
11. scientist
12. barber
13. butcher
14. mechanic
15. salesperson
16. gardener
17. carpenter
18. newscaster

B. LISTENING: *WHO'S TALKING?*

Listen and decide who is talking.

1. We'll be landing in just a few minutes.
2. All right, class. Please turn to page fifty-three.
3. I can't remember my lines!
4. Good morning. Dr. Brown's office. May I help you?
5. Where do you want me to let you off?
6. I think you'll really like this apartment.
7. You won't believe what I've just caught!
8. How about Hawaii? That would be a nice place for a vacation.
9. I'll be over with the pizza you ordered in fifteen minutes.
10. Where should I put the laundry detergent?

11. Let me look at your paw, Rover.
12. What would you like for dessert?
13. I just bought seven new cows.
14. Here's your change—thirty-nine cents. Thank you, and have a nice day!
15. You're under arrest!

Answers

3	1	5
14	15	2
9	6	8
13	4	11
7	10	12

C. ANALOGIES

1. hairdresser
2. artist
3. mechanic
4. veterinarian
5. carpenter
6. construction worker
7. bus driver
8. butcher
9. real estate
10. pharmacist
11. actress
12. plumber
13. courier

D. LIKELY OR UNLIKELY?

	Likely	Unlikely
1.		✔
2.	✔	
3.		✔
4.	✔	
5.		✔
6.		✔
7.	✔	
8.		✔
9.	✔	
10.		✔
11.		✔
12.		✔
13.	✔	
14.	✔	
15.		✔
16.		✔
17.		✔
18.		✔

WORKBOOK PAGES 86–87

A. WHAT'S THE ACTION?

1. play
2. operate
3. file
4. act
5. translate
6. wash
7. deliver
8. serve
9. write
10. bake
11. paint
12. sing
13. type
14. draw
15. sew
16. grow
17. drive
18. repair
19. guard
20. teach
21. assemble
22. build
23. design
24. cook
25. fly
26. sell
27. mow
28. clean

B. WHAT DO THEY HAVE IN COMMON?

1. d
2. e
3. a
4. c
5. f
6. h
7. b
8. g

C. WHAT'S THE CATEGORY?

1. cook
2. wash
3. grow
4. play
5. bake
6. build/design
7. fly
8. write
9. serve
10. teach
11. drive
12. paint
13. deliver
14. guard
15. repair/fix

WORKBOOK PAGE 88

A. WHICH WORD IS CORRECT?

1. coat rack
2. conference room
3. reception area
4. machine
5. typist
6. receptionist
7. supply cabinet
8. office manager
9. copier
10. storage room

B. LISTENING: *WHAT'S THE LAST WORD?*

Listen and complete the sentences.

1. I'm using the copy . . . .
2. I'll meet you in the reception . . . .
3. You can hang your coat in the coat . . . .
4. You can find that report in the file . . . .
5. Maria is busy at her work . . . .
6. Where's the postage . . . ?
7. We'll be meeting in the conference . . . .
8. Bob is taking a break. He's in the employee . . . .
9. Tina works part-time as a file . . . .
10. Ms. Walters is our new administrative . . .

Answers

8	3	6	2	9
5	4	7	10	1

C. LISTENING: *WHERE ARE THEY?*

Listen and decide where the conversation is taking place.

1. A. These are coming out too light.
   B. You're right. Something must be wrong with the machine.

2. A. Is this the Bradley Corporation?
   B. No. The Bradley Corporation is on the next floor.
   A. Thanks.

3. A. Please put this letter in Ms. Crane's box. It's the second one down on the left.
   B. Certainly.

4. A. Let's see. Glue. Where do you think it might be?
   B. Look over there on the third shelf.

5. I glad you could all come to this important meeting today.

6. A. It's ten thirty. We'd better get back to work.
   B. You're right.

Answers

2
5
4
6
1
3

D. LISTENING: *WHO'S TALKING?*

Listen and decide who is talking.

1. I'm upset. I've already made several mistakes in this letter.
2. I can't remember where I put the McDonald folder—under M or under D.
3. I know every employee who works for me.
4. Welcome to the Sterling Company!
5. I'm going to deliver the mail now.

Answers

3	1	4	2	5

WORKBOOK PAGES 89–90

A. WHAT'S THE WORD?
1. telephone, phone system
2. postal scale
3. paper cutter
4. calculator
5. microcassette recorder/dictaphone
6. pencil sharpener
7. plastic binding machine
8. laser printer
9. typewriter, computer/word processor
10. letter-quality printer
11. fax machine
12. computer/word processor
13. paper shredder

B. WHICH CAME FIRST?
1. pencil sharpeners
2. adding machines
3. typewriters
4. telex machines
5. dot-matrix printers

C. OFFICE ASSOCIATIONS
1. c, d, f
2. c
3. d, f
4. a, e
5. d, f
6. d, f
7. b, g
8. d, f
9. a, e

D. LISTENING: *WHAT ARE THEY TALKING ABOUT?*
Listen and decide what office item is being talked about.
1. This is the best quality printer you can buy.
2. It's amazing! Just dial the number and in a few seconds, you can send a letter anywhere in the world!
3. It's not an electric one, but it still works very well.
4. Don't forget to use this to weigh the letter before you mail it.
5. Let me have it and I'll compute the answer in just a second.
6. This will cut the paper to just the size you want it.

Answers
1. b
2. a
3. a
4. a
5. b
6. b

WORKBOOK PAGE 91

A. JANET'S NEW OFFICE
1. desk
2. letter opener
3. pencil cup
4. rolodex
5. letter tray/stacking stray
6. paper clip dispenser
7. appointment book
8. tape dispenser
9. memo holder
10. organizer/personal planner
11. highlighter (pen)
12. scissors
13. desk calendar, wall calendar
14. nameplate
15. wastebasket

B. A GOOD IDEA!/NOT A GOOD IDEA!

	A Good Idea	Not a Good Idea
1.	✔	
2.		✔
3.		✔
4.	✔	
5.	✔	
6.		✔

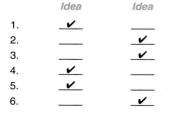

C. LISTENING: *WHAT ARE THEY TALKING ABOUT?*
Listen and decide what's being talked about.
1. I really enjoy sitting on it.
2. It isn't bright enough.
3. It just ran out of lead. It won't write!
4. That's where I write down all my meetings.
5. I put my papers together with this.
6. This is where I keep people's names, addresses, and phone numbers.
7. You make holes with this.
8. I give one to every client I meet.
9. You correct your mistakes with this.

Answers
1. b
2. b
3. b
4. a
5. a
6. b
7. b
8. a
9. b

WORKBOOK PAGE 92

A. WHAT AM I?
1. typing paper
2. carbon paper
3. correction fluid
4. mailing label
5. Post-It note pad
6. rubber band
7. computer paper
8. legal pad
9. Scotch tape/cellophane tape

B. WHAT'S THE WORD?
1. stationery
2. typewriter ribbon
3. mailer
4. index card
5. mailing label
6. package mailing tape
7. gluestick
8. thumbtack

WORKBOOK PAGE 93

A. ASSOCIATIONS
1. g
2. a
3. e
4. i
5. d
6. b
7. f
8. c
9. h
10. j

B. WHAT'S THE WORD?
1. lever
2. payroll office
3. supply room
4. loading dock
5. safety glasses
6. suggestion box
7. fire extinguisher
8. freight elevator
9. quality control supervisor
10. first-aid kit

WORKBOOK PAGE 94

A. WHAT'S THE OBJECT?
1. d
2. a
3. f
4. e
5. b
6. c

B. WHAT'S THE WORD?
1. blueprints
2. ladder
3. insulation
4. bulldozer, dump truck
5. pipe
6. toolbelt
7. tape measure
8. hard hat
9. plywood, lumber
10. jackhammer
11. scaffolding
12. brick
13. shingle

WORKBOOK PAGES 95–96

A. LISTENING: *CALLING ABOUT A CAR*
Listen to the following telephone conversation and circle the answers as you listen.
A. Hi. I'm calling about the ad for the seven hundred dollar car. Is it still for sale?
B. Yes, it is.
A. What kind of car is it?

B. It's a Ford hatchback in almost perfect condition.
A. Almost perfect?
B. Well, it has a few minor problems.
A. A few minor problems?
B. Yes. It needs a new fan belt.
A. Oh, that's no problem at all.
B. Well, uh . . . we're also having a little trouble with the transmission. The fact of the matter is, it may need a new clutch.
A. I see. Tell me, is there anything else wrong with the car?
B. Well, as a matter of fact, the battery is a bit old.
A. I see.
B. And it probably wouldn't hurt to get a new air filter while you're at it.
A. A new air filter?
B. Yes. And I suppose it wouldn't hurt to have the alternator checked.
A. The alternator?
B. Yes. Oh. And incidentally, the brakes are squeaking . . . just a little. But those are minor things. And aside from the little problem with the gas gauge and the defroster, everything is really in tip-top shape!
A. What's wrong with the gas gauge and the defroster?
B. They don't work.
A. I see. Tell me, does ANYTHING in the car work?
B. Oh, yes. The horn and the warning lights work fine!

Answers

1. a	6. b
2. b	7. a
3. b	8. a
4. a	9. b
5. b	10. a

B. WHICH WORD IS CORRECT?

1. speedometer	7. bumper
2. hood, dipstick	8. trunk
3. ignition	9. radiator
4. stickshift, clutch	10. station
5. windshield wipers, rear defroster	11. nozzle, gas
6. taillight	12. emergency brake

C. CROSSWORD PUZZLE

See page 155.

WORKBOOK PAGE 97

A. A GOOD IDEA!/NOT A GOOD IDEA!

	A Good Idea	Not a Good Idea
1.		✔
2.		✔
3.	✔	
4.	✔	
5.		✔
6.		✔
7.	✔	
8.		✔
9.		✔
10.	✔	
11.		✔
12.	✔	
13.		✔
14.	✔	
15.	✔	
16.		✔
17.	✔	
18.		✔

B. LISTENING TO DIRECTIONS

Listen and fill in the missing directional information.

A. Good morning. This is ESL-To-Go! How may I help you?
B. I'm registered for your one-day intensive English course for beginners, and I'm calling for directions from Centerville.
A. Do you have a pencil and paper?
B. Yes, I do.
A. Okay. Take the interstate north. After you pass a rest area, you'll see signs for Flagstaff. Get in the right lane and take Exit Six. The exit sign says Maple Street. Are you with me so far?
B. Yes. I'm with you.
A. You'll immediately go through a school crossing and will have to slow down. At the next intersection, there's a stop sign. Go straight, cross over a railroad crossing, and then take your next right onto a one-way street. You'll cross a small bridge, and we're located at the first corner on the right. There's a large sign out front. Did you get all that?
B. Yes, I did.
A. Then I don't think you should be in our beginning-level course. How about our one-day advanced level class?!

Answers

1. interstate	4. school crossing
2. rest area	5. one-way street
3. right, six	6. bridge, corner

WORKBOOK PAGE 98

DIRECTIONS TO MY HOUSE

1. baggage	10. schedule
2. bus stop	11. arrival and departure board
3. bus	12. track
4. subway station	13. Porters
5. token	14. conductor
6. token booth	15. taxicab
7. turnstile	16. fare
8. train station	17. meter
9. ticket window	18. cab driver

WORKBOOK PAGE 99

A. A FRUSTRATING FLIGHT!

1. ticket counter	9. boarding pass
2. ticket agent	10. waiting area
3. arrival and departure monitor	11. gate
4. security checkpoint	12. customs
5. X-ray machine	13. customs declaration form
6. metal detector	14. passport
7. security guard	15. baggage claim area
8. check-in	16. (baggage) claim check

B. ANALOGIES

1. concession stand	4. boarding pass
2. ticket agent	5. baggage carousel
3. Gate	baggage claim (area)

WORKBOOK PAGE 100

A. PROBABLE OR IMPROBABLE?

1. I	8. P
2. I	9. I
3. P	10. I
4. P	11. I
5. I	12. P
6. I	13. P
7. I	14. I

B. WHICH WORD DOESN'T BELONG?

1. instrument panel (The others are people.)
2. armrest (The others are above the seat.)
3. cargo door (The others are associated with emergences.)
4. seat belt (The others are seat locations.)

5. jet (The others are parts of a plane.)
6. rotor (The others are types of planes.)
7. galley (The others are people.)

C. WHICH WORD?

1. pilot
2. seat belt
3. compartment
4. tail
5. cabin
6. cockpit

WORKBOOK PAGE 101

A. WEATHER TALK

1. sunny
2. drizzling
3. cloudy
4. muggy
5. snowstorm
6. thunderstorm
7. hurricane
8. lightning
9. foggy

B. A GOOD IDEA!/NOT A GOOD IDEA!

1. a
2. b
3. a
4. b
5. b
6. b
7. a
8. a
9. b
10. b
11. b

WORKBOOK PAGE 102

A. ASSOCIATIONS

1. c
2. g
3. i
4. a
5. h
6. e
7. d
8. b
9. f

B. LISTENING

Listen and choose the best answer.

1. We'd like to sit, but the grass is a little damp. Let's spread out the . . . .
2. We're going on a picnic and I need something to put the juice in. Can I borrow your . . . ?
3. It's a beautiful night. The sky is filled with stars. Let's sleep outside in our . . . .
4. I have no idea where this trail ends. I wish you hadn't forgotten the . . . !
5. Believe it or not, some hikers carry as much as sixty pounds of supplies and provisions in their . . . .
6. We could make a clothesline between these two trees if we had some . . . .
7. We could boil water without building a fire if only we had a . . . .
8. We can't put up the tent because we can't find the . . . .
9. I have no idea where north is because I dropped the . . . !

Answers

5	1	8
7	6	2
9	3	4

C. THE RIGHT RESPONSE

1. f
2. b
3. c
4. h
5. d
6. g
7. e
8. a
9. i

A. WHAT'S THE WORD?

1. picnic area
2. band shell
3. jogging path, bridle path
4. trash can
5. wading pool
6. statue
7. merry-go-round
8. rest room
9. water fountain
10. bike rack
11. zoo
12. monkey bars, playground
13. sand, sandbox

B. LISTENING: WHERE ARE THEY?

Listen and decide where these people are.

1. A. What a great concert!
   B. I agree.
2. A. Hey! Let's go on the slide!
   B. Great idea!
3. A. How long have we been running?
   B. For over twenty minutes.
4. A. What did you bring?
   B. Some sandwiches, some drinks, and some fruit.
5. A. Which horse do you want to sit on?
   B. The green and red one over there.
6. A. How long have we been riding?
   B. For a long time. Let's stop. I think my horse is getting tired.

Answers

| 3 | 4 | 5 |
| 2 | 6 | 1 |

WORKBOOK PAGES 104–105

A. CAN YOU FIND . . . ?

Things to sit or lie on:	People at the beach:	Things to protect you from the sun:
beach chair	lifeguard	beach umbrella
blanket	sunbather	sun hat
lifeguard stand	surfer	sunglasses
towel	swimmer	suntan lotion/ sunscreen
	vendor	

Beach toys:	Things we use in the water:	Things we wear or put on:
beach ball	air mattress/ raft	bathing cap
kite	kickboard	bathing suit/ swimsuit
pail/bucket	surfboard	sun hat
shovel	tube	sunglasses

B. WHICH WORD IS CORRECT?

1. towel
2. bathing cap
3. beach umbrella
4. seashells
5. cooler
6. lifeguard, swimmers
7. surfboard
8. snack bar
9. lifeguard stand
10. sand dunes
11. kickboard
12. kite
13. sunglasses
14. waves
15. ball
16. swimsuit

C. WHAT'S THE OBJECT?

1. e
2. g
3. h
4. b
5. c
6. a
7. f
8. d

149

D. WHAT'S THE ACTION?

1. f		6. a	
2. c		7. h	
3. e		8. d	
4. i		9. b	
5. g			

E. LIKELY OR UNLIKELY?

	Likely	Unlikely
1.	___	✔
2.	✔	___
3.	✔	___
4.	___	✔
5.	___	✔
6.	✔	___
7.	✔	___
8.	___	✔
9.	✔	___
10.	___	✔
11.	✔	___

WORKBOOK PAGES 106–107

A. "OUT OF PLACE"

1. running
   skateboarding
2. bowling
   karate
3. frisbee
   golf
4. weightlifting
   cycling
5. golf
   skateboarding
   skydiving
6. handball
   darts
7. roller skating
   running
   racquetball

B. ANALOGIES

1. paddle
2. pool stick
3. (boxing) trunks
4. (bicycle) helmet
5. elbow pads

C. WHAT AM I?

1. trampoline
2. parachute
3. squash
4. target

D. NAME THAT SPORT!

1. bowling
2. skydiving
3. billiards/pool
   golf
4. cycling/bicycling/biking
   roller skating
   skateboarding
5. wrestling
6. boxing
7. handball
   racquetball
   squash
8. karate
9. golf
10. exercise bike

WORKBOOK PAGE 108

A. CORRECT OR INCORRECT?

1. I		5. C	
2. I		6. C	
3. C		7. C	
4. I		8. I	

B. TRUE OR FALSE?

1. F		4. F	
2. T		5. F	
3. T			

C. SEARCH FOR THE ANSWER

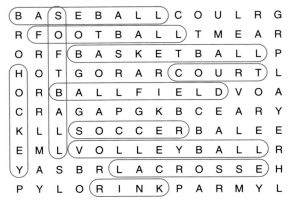

1. Baseball
2. softball, ballfield
3. **soccer, football**
4. Hockey, rink
5. Basketball, court
6. Volleyball
7. lacrosse

WORKBOOK PAGE 109

A. SENSE OR NONSENSE?

	Sense	Nonsense
1.	___	✔
2.	✔	___
3.	✔	___
4.	___	✔
5.	___	✔
6.	✔	___
7.	___	✔
8.	___	✔

B. WHO'S TALKING?

1. c		5. g	
2. d		6. b	
3. a		7. e	
4. f			

C. LISTENING

Listen and decide which answer is correct.

1. Please look for my softball . . . .
2. He hit the back . . . .
3. Every volleyball player knows you can't touch the . . . .
4. It's my turn to bat. I need a . . . .
5. Bob is an excellent skater. He should try out for the . . . .
6. A basketball is much larger than a . . . .
7. Football players need to wear . . . .
8. Our team has the best-looking . . . .

ANSWERS

1. b		5. b	
2. a		6. a	
3. b		7. b	
4. a		8. a	

WORKBOOK PAGE 110

A. WHAT'S THE OBJECT?

1. d		5. c	
2. b		6. a	
3. g		7. e	
4. f			

B. WHAT'S THE SPORT?

1. (downhill) skiing, cross-country skiing
2. (ice) skating

3. (downhill) skiing, sledding, toboganning
4. (downhill) skiing, (ice) skating, figure skating
5. (ice) skating, figure skating
6. (downhill) skiing
7. sledding, (downhill) skiing, toboganning
8. snowmobiling

WORKBOOK PAGE 111

A. ASSOCIATIONS

1. f	6. a
2. e	7. d
3. b	8. i
4. g	9. c
5. h	

B. WHAT DO YOU WEAR?

1. c	4. a
2. e	5. b
3. f	6. d

C. WHAT'S THE SPORT?

1. b	5. e
2. c	6. d
3. a	7. h
4. f	8. g

WORKBOOK PAGE 112

A. WHAT DO YOU DO?

1. c	4. d
2. e	5. a
3. f	6. b

B. WHAT'S THE ACTION?

1. shoot	7. hop
2. kick	8. bend
3. bounce	9. reach
4. catch, pitch	10. swim, dive
5. serve	11. Stretch
6. run	

WORKBOOK PAGE 113

WHAT'S THE WORD?

1. painting	10. bird watching
2. sewing	11. Monopoly
3. knitting	12. model building
4. weaving	13. stamp collecting
5. crocheting	14. astronomy
6. woodworking	15. photography
7. pottery	16. cards
8. sculpting	17. Chess
9. coin collecting	

WORKBOOK PAGE 114

A. WHAT'S HAPPENING THIS WEEKEND?

1. stage	8. Ticket
2. theater	9. balcony
3. audience	10. box office
4. scenery	11. ballet company
5. lighting	12. ballet dancer
6. actor	13. conductor
7. actress	14. lobby

B. LISTENING

Listen and choose the best answer.

1. The audience gave Maria Rossini a standing ovation the minute she stepped into the . . . .
2. Did you know that Richard Hallmark played the lead role in several other productions? I saw it here in the . . . .
3. The movie was so powerful that even after it ended, many people sat and continued to sit and stare at the . . . .
4. In the last scene, the lead singer sings the closing song along with the entire . . . .
5. We had wonderful seats at the ballet last night. We sat in the . . . .
6. All the musicians rose to their feet when the conductor stepped up to the . . . .
7. I think I'll get some popcorn at the . . . .
8. You need to show your ticket to the . . . .

Answers

1. a	5. b
2. b	6. b
3. b	7. a
4. a	8. b

WORKBOOK PAGES 115–116

A. WHAT'S ON TV?

1. news program
   (. . . . .)
2. cartoon
   (. . . . .)
3. drama
   (. . . . .)
4. game show
   (. . . . .)
5. talk show
   (. . . . .)
6. sitcom
   (. . . . .)
7. sports program
   (. . . . .)
8. children's program
   (. . . . .)

B. WHAT'S AT THE MOVIES?

1. western	5. war movie
2. science fiction movie	6. drama
3. foreign film	7. comedy
4. cartoon	8. adventure movie

C. LISTENING

Listen and put a number next to the type of music you hear.

1. (classical music)	6. (reggae)
2. (rock music)	7. (blues)
3. (country music)	8. (gospel music)
4. (jazz)	9. (rap music)
5. (folk music)	

Answers

8	1	6
2	3	9
5	7	4

WORKBOOK PAGE 117

A. WHICH INSTRUMENT DOESN'T BELONG?

1. drum (The others are string instruments.)
2. accordion (The others are percussion instruments.)
3. banjo (The others are brass instruments.)
4. cello (The others are woodwinds.)
5. bassoon (The others are keyboard instruments.)

B. LIKELY OR UNLIKELY?

	Likely	Unlikely
1.		✔
2.		✔
3.	✔	
4.		✔
5.	✔	
6.		✔
7.	✔	
8.		✔

C. ASSOCIATIONS

1. f
2. d
3. g
4. a

5. b
6. e
7. c

D. LISTENING: *WHAT'S THAT SOUND?*

Listen and decide what musical instrument you're listening to.

1. (violin)
2. (organ)
3. (guitar)
4. (flute)
5. (piano)

6. (drums)
7. (harmonica)
8. (trumpet)
9. (cymbals)

Answers

5	7	8
6	9	2
4	1	3

WORKBOOK PAGES 118–119

A. CATEGORIES

Parts of a flower:

bud
petal
stamen
stem

Parts of a tree:

bark
leaf
limb
trunk

Types of flowers:

daffodil
daisy
petunia
tulip

Types of trees:

birch
cherry
maple
oak

B. WHAT AM I?

1. poison ivy
2. rose
3. weeping willow
4. bud
5. grass
6. palm tree
7. thorn
8. redwood

9. daffodil
10. orchid
11. daisy
12. pine
13. bulb
14. cactus
15. ivy

WORKBOOK PAGE 120

A. MATCH

1. f
2. l
3. k
4. e
5. g
6. j

7. d
8. h
9. b
10. c
11. a
12. i

B. WHICH WORD IS CORRECT?

1. forest
2. rapids
3. stream
4. seashore
5. cliffs

6. jungle
7. natural gas
8. waterfall
9. desert
10. pollution

LISTENING

Listen and choose the best answer.

1. One of the most serious international problems in this century is . . . .
2. I personally am very concerned about the disposal of . . . .
3. Two important energy sources are . . . .
4. A realistic alternative energy source is . . . .
5. One of the dangers of nuclear energy is the possible leaking of . . . .
6. Our lakes and streams are being contaminated by . . . .
7. The Middle East and parts of South America are rich sources of . . . .
8. One reason for the deterioration of the ozone layer is the burning of . . . .

Answers

1. a
2. b
3. a
4. b

5. b
6. b
7. a
8. b

WORKBOOK PAGES 121–122

A. WHERE ARE THEY?

1. farmhouse
2. coop
3. stable
4. garden

5. sty
6. orchard
7. henhouse
8. field

B. WHICH WORD IS CORRECT?

1. hired hand
2. irrigation system
3. combine
4. scarecrow
5. pitchfork

6. crop
7. pasture
8. farmhouse
9. barnyard
10. calves

C. ANIMAL SOUNDS!

1. d
2. f
3. b

4. c
5. e
6. a

D. CATEGORIES

Buildings:	Areas:	Machinery:
barn	barnyard	combine
chicken coop	field	tractor
farmhouse	orchard	
hen house	pasture	
silo	pigpen/pig sty	
stable	(vegetable) garden	

E. ANALOGIES

1. goat
2. hay
3. chicken coop
4. field

5. cow
6. sheep
7. calves
8. chickens/hens

F. WHO'S MY MOTHER?

1. pig
2. chicken
3. sheep

4. cow
5. horse
6. goat

G. ASSOCIATIONS

1. f
2. e
3. c
4. a

5. g
6. b
7. d

WORKBOOK PAGE 123

A. ANALOGIES

1. elephant
2. leopard
3. camel

4. fawn
5. wolves
6. mane

B. WHO'S TALKING?

1. giraffe
2. pony
3. dog
4. porcupine
5. lion
6. bat
7. skunk
8. moose

9. polar bear
10. worm
11. kangaroo
12. hyena
13. camel
14. cat
15. beaver

C. ANIMAL EXPRESSIONS

1. fox
2. mouse
3. donkey
4. horse
5. beaver
6. bat

WORKBOOK PAGE 124

A. COLOR ME BEAUTIFUL!

1. f
2. g
3. b
4. e
5. a
6. c
7. d

B. WHO'S TALKING?

1. termite
2. eagle
3. ladybug
4. firefly
5. wasp
6. flea
7. ostrich
8. robin
9. pigeon
10. seagull
11. praying mantis
12. stork
13. butterfly
14. beetle

WORKBOOK PAGE 125

A. ASSOCIATIONS

1. b
2. d
3. f
4. e
5. c
6. a

B. WHICH WORD DOESN'T BELONG?

1. scallop (The others are types of amphibians.)
2. clam (The others are parts of a sea animal.)
3. tadpole (The others are types of snakes.)
4. squid (The others are types of fish.)
5. eel (The others are types of sea animals.)
6. shell (The others are parts of a fish.)
7. snail (The others are large.)

C. LISTENING: *AT THE AQUARIUM*

Listen and circle the correct answer.

Welcome to the Centerville Aquarium! We hope you find your visit here today fun as well as educational. Down on the lower level, you can watch otters and walruses as they go about their daily routines in our authentic ocean tank. This large tank in the middle of the aquarium is specially constructed so you can view its inhabitants from all levels by walking up and down the ramp. In here you can see salmon, eels, swordfish, and tortoises. You can also see the fish with probably the worst reputation—sharks. People are generally frightened of sharks, but in fact, the only type of shark known to attack without provocation is also the kind you're least likely to come across—the *Great White Shark*. You'll also see striped bass and flounder here in the tank.

Can you tell the difference between crocodiles and alligators? Many people mix them up. Currently, we have a special exhibit highlighting the differences between them. Come to the exhibit on the second floor.

And while you're on the second floor, come to our tide pool, where children are actually encouraged to get their hands wet! You can examine starfish, snails, and jellyfish, as well as mussels, clams, oysters, scallops, and eels.

In our smaller tanks, we have crabs and lobsters, and be sure not to miss the special octopus tank nearby.

And after you've finished your tour, come and enjoy our dolphin, seal, and whale show. Kids and adults alike will just love it! Shows are on the hour, but get there early! They fill up fast!

We sincerely hope you enjoy your day today here at the Centerville Aquarium!

Answers

1. b
2. a
3. b
4. b
5. a
6. b
7. a

WORKBOOK PAGE 126

A. 3-D

1. cube
2. pyramid
3. cylinder
4. cone
5. sphere

B. WHAT'S THE WORD?

1. inches
2. kilometers
3. distance, miles
4. centimeters
5. yard
6. ellipse/oval
7. apex
8. isosceles
9. rectangle
10. hypotenuse

WORKBOOK PAGES 127–128

A. OUTER SPACE RIDDLES

1. n
2. c
3. d
4. f
5. e
6. h
7. i
8. o
9. p
10. k
11. j
12. b
13. g
14. a
15. m
16. l

B. SPACE EXPLORATION CROSSWORD PUZZLE

See page 156.

WORKBOOK PAGE 23

C. CROSSWORD PUZZLE

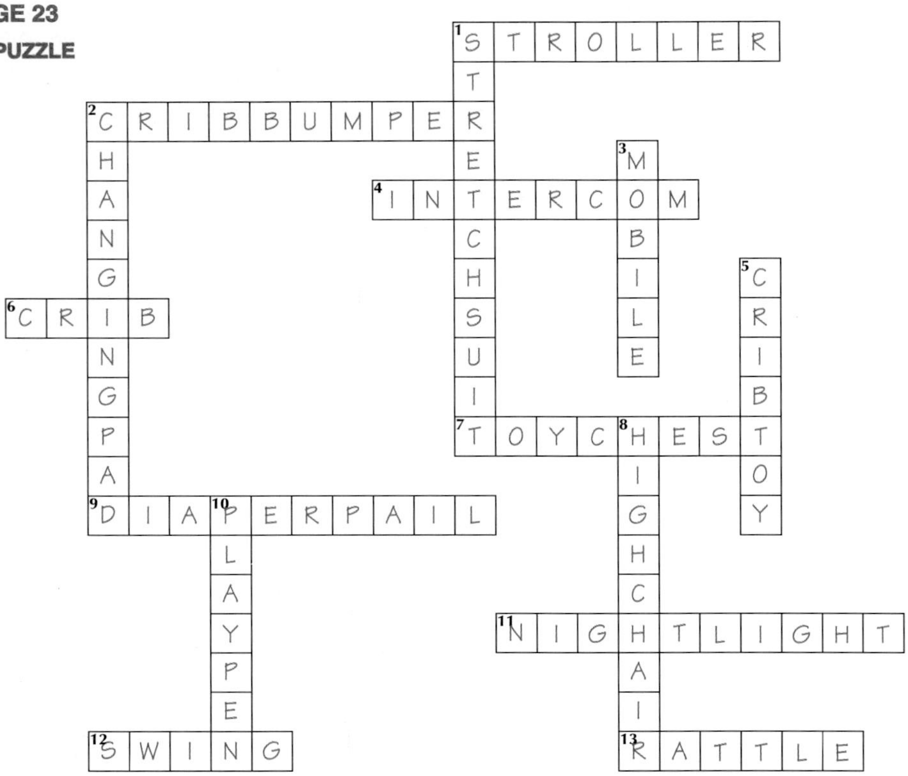
1 STROLLER
1 STRETCHSUIT
2 CRIBBUMPER
2 CHANGINGPAD
3 MOBILE
4 INTERCOM
5 CRIBTOY
6 CRIB
7 TOYCHEST
8 HIGHCHAIR
9 DIAPERPAIL
10 PLAYPEN
11 NIGHTLIGHT
12 SWING
13 RATTLE

WORKBOOK PAGE 35

C. CROSSWORD PUZZLE

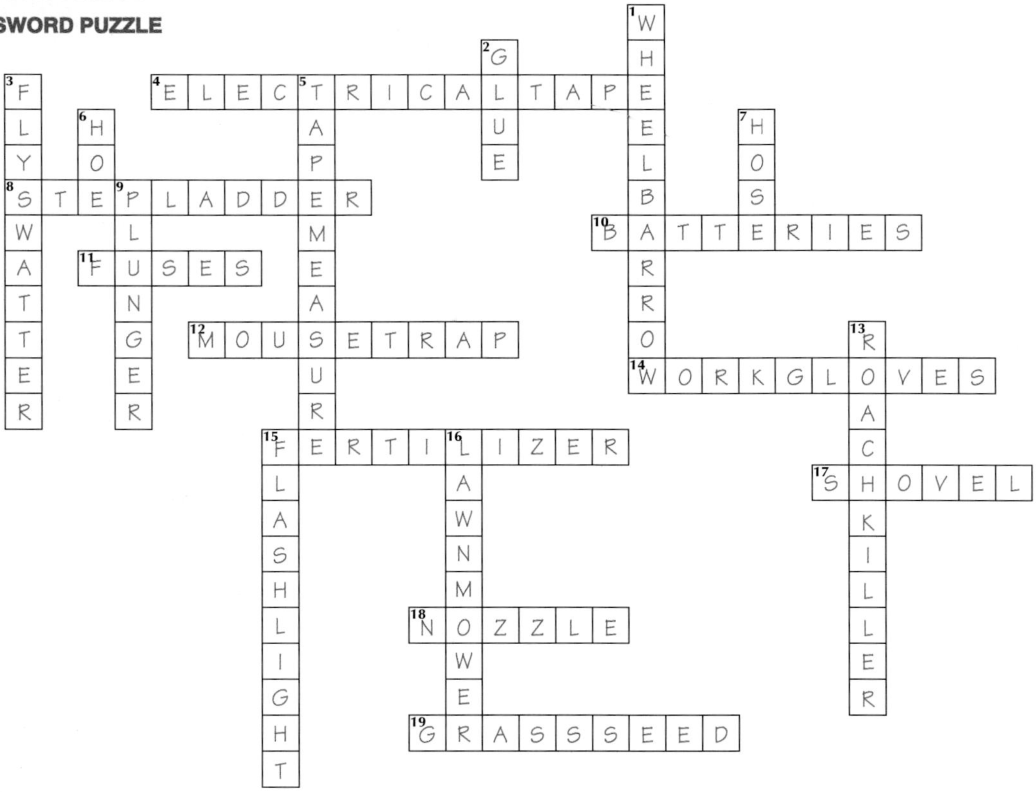
1 WHEELBARROW
2 GLUE
3 FLYSWATTER
4 ELECTRICALTAPE
5 TAPEMEASURE
6 HOE
7 HOSE
8 STEPLADDER
9 PLUNGER
10 BATTERIES
11 FUSES
12 MOUSETRAP
13 ROACHKILLER
14 WORKGLOVES
15 FERTILIZER
15 FLASHLIGHT
16 LAWNMOWER
17 SHOVEL
18 NOZZLE
19 GRASSSEED

A. CROSSWORD PUZZLE

C. CROSSWORD PUZZLE

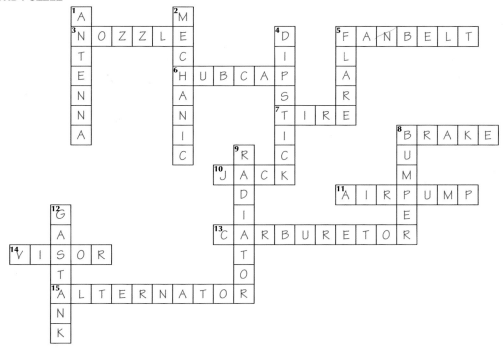

B. CROSSWORD PUZZLE

Across:
2. MISSION CONTROL
3. SPACE SHUTTLE
5. LAUNCH PAD
7. ORBITER
10. SPACE SUIT
11. UFO

Down:
1. BOOSTER ROCKET
4. SATELLITE
6. PROBE
8. ROCKET
9. ASTRONAUT